REVIEWS

TITLE INFORMATION

HOW TO DEVELOP A WINNING SELF-IMAGE
A Psychology of Personal Growth and Development
David A. Joyette
FriesenPress (147 pp.)

BOOK REVIEW

A debut manual offers advice on reprogramming inner attitudes about succeeding in life.

Joyette's slim handbook starts with an appealingly functional premise: that people approach the world's challenges in ways largely determined by their early upbringings and personal "programming." The author maintains that individuals can change this programming if they work at it (and, of course, consider the thoughts and guidelines laid out in this volume). Joyette wants his readers to ask themselves some disarmingly simple questions: What explanations do you have for the way your life currently is, and if it isn't to your liking, why is that? What are the factors that have gone into making your life and personality the way they are? The central contention of these pages is that most of the answers to such questions lie inside individuals— and are under their control if they'll only free themselves from negative, self-limiting thinking. "It is incredible," Joyette sarcastically notes, "how expert we become at 'knowing' what we can and cannot do." The essence of this inspirational book's teachings—presented in clear, highly kinetic prose—is that such expertise is often a self-fulfilling prophecy, the product of letting all of life's negative stimuli pile up and harden into a crust of self-defeat. The author's advice examines many personal improvement topics, always distinguishing between inner and outer enhancements—and emphasizing that the former is more important. On the subject of physical appearance, for instance, he advises modifying it in positive ways. But he stresses that the crucial second step is to "internalize positive beliefs" about appearance rather than tying self-esteem directly to it ("If you attach your self-worth in any way to how you look, and you aren't satisfied with what you look like, you're setting yourself up to be miserable"). Joyette includes a particularly blunt and enlightening chapter on how to apply these self-image improvement techniques when one is black in America—a subset frequently plagued with its own challenges, which the author addresses with plainspoken sensitivity.

A lean but surprisingly comprehensive guide that skillfully tells readers how to analyze and take control of their self-images.

EXCERPTING POLICIES

Kirkus Indie, Kirkus Media LLC, 6411 Burleson Rd., Austin, TX 78744
indie@kirkusreviews.com

HOW TO DEVELOP A
WINNING
SELF-IMAGE

A Psychology of Personal
Growth and development

Dr. David
A. Joyette

 FriesenPress

Suite 300 - 990 Fort St
Victoria, BC, V8V 3K2
Canada

www.friesenpress.com

ISBN
978-1-5255-2416-5 (Hardcover)
978-1-5255-2417-2 (Paperback)
978-1-5255-2418-9 (eBook)

1. *SELF-HELP*

Distributed to the trade by The Ingram Book Company

Table of Contents

This book is dedicated to my parents, Princes Etherline and Ormiston Leo Joyette, who have tirelessly planted noble seeds of wisdom in my mind, with words that have influenced my life, such as **"You are here in this world to do one thing and that is to learn. As you learn, you will grow, and as you grow, you will change... There will always be changes."**

Preface

Many years ago, after graduating from college, we were living in a suburb of Toronto. My wife and I decided to take a drive to the city's downtown core. We parked our car, and were determined to explore the city's downtown and take in scenes of Gothic and modern architecture by foot. While doing this, we discovered that, in many areas, there were pan-handlers and the homeless. Speaking with some of them, I realized that many had mental-health issues, while others were social misfits and outcasts in our society. This presented me with a great and unique opportunity to delve into the question, "Why are men poor?" It was not long before I realized that being poor was a state of mind … called poverty.

I began investigating the reasons for this malady. As the reasons unfolded, it became increasingly apparent that the basis lies in our programming—the conditioning we receive throughout our early lives, from infancy up to about the age of 10, which prepares us for the future. If this conditioning is positive, and we are influenced by it positively, we will be successful and look at the future with positive self-expectancy. On the other hand, if our programming was negative, or is perceived as negative, we will view the world as negative, and this will produce negative self-expectancy and low self-esteem.

In my endeavour to find a cure, my investigation took me back to my adolescence, my childhood, my infancy, my conception, and beyond, and it confirmed my suspicion that my programming (conditioning) was impaired, and had to be corrected if I were to be successful. I also found that retraining the mind was the only way to produce lasting results. In addition, I found that without a philosophy that reflects my truth, in terms of how I want to live, what I aim to be, and how to make choices that are right for me, I will be a failure. Without a philosophy, I will be living my life by other people's wishes. I will be following the crowd, as they walk off the cliff to their deaths. I did not want this to happen, so I charted a course for my success that includes my family's success.

I created a success path—a path that will show results—focusing on five basic questions, and the short answers to them.

1. Who am I? This took about one week, regressing through my life's path and pulling valuable themes from my history.

2. Why am I here? This took about three days, gleaming information from my personality to see how my subjectivity fits with what society offers.

3. Where am I going from here? I wanted to be of service to others—the poor and downtrodden. This took a week, investigating all the career paths to see what met society's needs and my own.

4. What vehicle will take me there? I chose Medicine, but soon realized it was not a fit, because of my poor attitude towards others.

5. When I get there, what will I do? This is still a work in progress. To sharpen my thinking and application skills, I spend my time reading and digesting the writings of Gandhi, William James, Kagan, Frankl, Carl Jung, Henry David Thoreau, and many others in the field of psychology and human development. Through this, I was able to use many vehicles to influence the minds, attitudes, and behaviours of others, help them to look at the world with both positive and negative values, and to learn from their mistakes and the misrepresentations of their life's path. Whether by teaching, lecturing, or experiential exercises, they are designed to change lives. These vehicles also had a great impact on influencing and changing me. The following incidents cemented in me the knowledge that "behavioural changes are real" if we are determined to see and feel the positive results of our actions.

The day after our wedding, I remembered discussing logically and rationally what expectations I had for our marriage—my vision for successful nuptials with my wife. We reasoned it out and agreed on a plan of action for the future, including having children. We articulated how and where we would live, how our children would be reared, what school they would be attending, and what plans we had for their future. But looking over our own history (both of us of Caribbean descent), we realized that, if our children were to grow in the direction of our desired choices, we had to undergo a metamorphosis of changes in our attitudes and behaviours. We, therefore, took courses in psychology and human development, and these (along with our determination) aided us in making gradual, incremental changes that continued for many years. We learned and grew from every step we took along our life path.

Here is the great problem facing young people: They are required, at a certain stage of their growth, to commit themselves to something and assume responsibility for the consequences. I remembered vividly, as if it were yesterday, taking both of my children to repair a house, about thirty-years ago. They were in their pre-teens, and while on a break, I decided to have them each take an oath to be the best son or daughter possible. I recited it to them, and began like this: "I (daughter) promise to be the best daughter possible, upholding the values, customs, and rules in our home and society, so help me God."

"I will, Daddy," she answered.

To my son, I said, "I (son) promise to be the best son possible, upholding the values, customs, and rules in our home and society, so help me God.

"I will, Daddy," he answered.

At this point, I startled both children when I, too, took the oath, promising to be the best parent possible, etc. To my amazement, both children hugged me around my waist and squeezed me, and then, like a choir singing, they muttered, "I love Daddy."

From that day on, there was a transformation of changes within the family. It blew my mind to notice the many positive changes and experiences that took place in our home. All because of the love we demonstrated for each other. This gave a sense of purpose and direction, and taught them that they were responsible for all their actions and decisions. By exposing (and making themselves aware of) their own ills, a better understanding of "self" would be gained. Instead of moping about my failures and life's problems, I have to think through my failures and life's problems to reach success. Success, to me, is and was what I say it is, and not what friends, associates, or society say it is. I must be a problem-solver ... not a problem.

A Winner's Image

"When the dream is big enough,
the facts don't matter."

Sam Kalenuik

The facts have never stood in the way of a WINNER. For WINNERS are dreamers who understand how to turn their dreams into reality, and in so doing, create a better, more beautiful world for everyone.

The facts may be real, and might represent strong opposition, but the facts don't matter to the winner—that person who holds in his heart a splendid image of his dream.

Throughout the ages, WINNERS have referred to a place within each of us called the higher self—that place where an image of perfection exists, which is continually attempting to express itself.

This higher self persistently sends stimulating and upbeat messages to our consciousness—messages which are meant to protect our integrity, and wholeness as creative beings. Messages coming from the heart always have a complete disregard for the facts or surrounding circumstances in our lives.

Unfortunately, 99 percent of people misread the signals they are continually receiving. Rather than viewing these images with their inner-eye of understanding, and seeing them as unique pictures packed with power, possibility, and promise, these images are considered idle wishes, ridiculous fantasies, or daydreams.

In *Man's search for meaning*, Victor Frankl said:

> "Everything can be taken from a person but one thing:
> the last of human freedoms—
> to choose one's attitude
> in any given set of circumstances...
> to choose one's own way."

Masses of people who struggle day in and day out permit their mind to be dominated by the facts—the lack of___, the limitations of___, the poverty that is reflected in their present RESULTS. They know why they can't win. It's obvious to them, and they can prove it. The facts win again and again.

If this is a description of your life, release it. Let it go. Begin doing what I will be suggesting, and your compensation will be worth the effort.

Chapter 1
Uncover New Freedom

Have you ever asked yourself why you are the way you are? If you're happy, then why are you happy? If you are successful, why are you successful? On the other hand, if you're frustrated and unhappy, then why are you frustrated and unhappy? Think for a moment, what explanation do you have for why your life is the way it is, and if it is less than you wish it were, why is that? These are all very important questions, because each of them invites us to look deep into our lives and evaluate how we view ourselves.

According to a Gallup poll, conducted in the early 80s, most people doing this would not like what they found. An astounding 66 percent of the people responding to the survey reported that they were not happy, and did not really see much hope or any major changes down the road. Yet everyone wants to be happy and fulfilled. But unfortunately, even with our modern conveniences, many people just aren't that satisfied with their lives. Why is this? You would think that, in this day and age, when people have more of everything, including freedom, possessions, money, leisure time, recreational outlets, and opportunities, they would be happier and more fulfilled and positive than ever. But they aren't. Why?

And what about you? Have you ever taken the time to pause and examine your own situation? Is your life progressing the way you'd always hoped it would, and if it isn't, have you really wondered why? Do you feel confident and hopeful that the future offers promise?

I'm reminded of a friend of mine who's continually coming up with all kinds of creative ways to make money. He's had ideas for books, inventions, machines, business investments, souvenirs, real-estate transactions, clubs, mail-order businesses, and an ongoing list of other ideas. You would think that someone with such a fertile imagination would be highly successful and rich. But this isn't the case. Although my friend is continually spewing out ideas like a volcano, he hasn't acted on a single one of them. He thinks about them, tells me about them, gets all excited, and even does prototypes. He brings me some of his inventions to show me. But after wishfully dreaming for a little while, he gives up without even trying. Instead of carrying through with those ideas, he spends his time thinking of all kinds of reasons why none of them will work. As an inventor, he sees himself as a failure. There's really no objective reason why he couldn't succeed with at least some of these ideas, but he doesn't even try. He mutters to his friends that it would be too expensive to develop, that it's difficult, that no one would probably buy it anyway, and it's too much trouble.

He does have tremendous ability. He's very talented, and is one of the most personable people I know. Yet he continually defeats himself even before getting started, because in his own mind, he has a strong image of failing. His self-image, like everyone else's, is limiting his life. This story illustrates what this whole topic is about. It's about your own best friend and your worst enemy: yourself. Like my friend, people become frustrated, unhappy, disillusioned, and discontented, not because they lack of ability or opportunity but because they limit their own happiness and success by creating barriers in their minds.

In almost every case, those barriers relate to internal pictures, thoughts, and beliefs they have about themselves. When people tell themselves, "I can't do that. I'm not smart enough. I will never reach my goals. I'm too shy. I can't succeed, because of this or that," they defeat themselves before ever getting started, and become their own worst enemies. Your own self-image and feelings of self-worth are the greatest forces in your life. They determine everything about you: your job, your financial condition, your family, your emotional well-being, your social status, your physical well-being, your relationships, and even the neighbourhood you live in. Your self-image actually determines the complete quality of your life.

You see, if you're not happy and fulfilled now, and if your life is not as you wish it were, the solution lies not in some external conditions, such as having more money, a better job, a more harmonious family, and more friends, but in the deepest, most heartfelt feelings and beliefs that you have about yourself as a person. You become what you think you already are. Your experiences in life are simply mirrors of your self-image and self-concept. You are now going to embark on an exciting journey of self-discovery. You will be taking an in-depth look into yourself, and analyzing your own self-concept for both positive and negative beliefs. No doors will be left closed. You will be opening the closet, revealing any skeletons that may be working there in the dark corners, and confronting them head-on. I'll be leading you through many different activities, including some written sessions, affirmations, visualizations, and relaxation sessions.

These sessions will assist you in adopting completely positive self-esteem, and self-image. Many will be centred around helping you release negative and limiting beliefs or concepts that you may have regarding your self-image. Others are geared to internalizing positive concepts and perceptions of yourself. You will be defining exactly how you view yourself now, and shaping that image to conform to your goal, your aspirations, your desires, and your dreams, and as the process unfolds, you will learn that you can achieve almost anything you want to achieve. You can become the kind of person you've always dreamed about being, and can be happy and fulfilled.

Now, there is no need to compromise any aspect of your life. The secret to this lies in a very little-understood power and influence that your self-image and self-esteem have over virtually every aspect of your life. The German philosopher Goethe wrote that the greatest evil that can possibly come before man is that he should come to think ill of himself. Goethe understood that a person's self-image can actually determine the kind of life he or she will have. If a person is filled with positive beliefs and expectancies concerning success, achievement, happiness, and fulfillment, the individual will more than likely have a very rich and rewarding life. But, on the other hand, if people see themselves as undeserving and limited in their capacity for success and fulfillment, their experiences will most probably fall far short of attaining the happiness and achievement they desire.

One psychologist said that self-esteem is the value without which no others are possible. It's the hallmark of mental health. The now legendary Mahatma Gandhi put it this way: Men often become what they believe themselves to be. If I believe I cannot do something, it makes me incapable of doing it, but when I believe I can, I acquire the ability to do it, even if I didn't have it in the beginning.

People act and perform in accordance with how they see themselves. As long as their mental pictures are success oriented, they will not find themselves facing any serious difficulties that can't be solved with a little work and perseverance. The problems happen when people form faulty self-images, flawed with any number of negative blocks and limitations of themselves. A negative self-concept can make it almost impossible for a person to get ahead in life and be happy and fulfilled, no matter how much ability or potential the person has, and no matter how hard he or she tries. This is because it is virtually impossible to act in conflict with your self-image. This is a very important concept to grasp. Once you come to understand how and why your self-image works to actually create the kind of person you want to be, you can then take the necessary steps to shape and mould your mind into a powerful force that will propel you toward fulfillment, happiness, and success. To fully comprehend how self-image can be so influential in your life, it's really important to understand just what is meant by the term.

Many would say that it is clear. It is simply how (and why) people see themselves in their mind, and while this is true, there's a whole lot more to it. First of all, a person's self-image operates on several levels. It's far more than just your conscious perceptions and beliefs about yourself. In fact, you'll soon learn that your conscious self-image isn't really the issue at all. If it were, then changing any negative belief would be as easy as saying, "Well, starting right now, I'm going to have a completely positive mental picture of myself. That's all it is to it." Unfortunately, it's not that simple, because the self-concept that exerts the most influence over you is housed in your sub-conscious mind, not your conscious mind.

Many people aren't even aware of what their subconscious self-images can do. We will be covering this extremely important aspect of self-image and self-esteem in detail later, when I get into the subject of the subconscious mind. I will be leading you through many different activities that will enable you to work directly with it, but for now, the important thing for you to understand is that your self-image stems primarily from the beliefs and perceptions in your *subconscious* mind. Secondly, getting an accurate portrayal of your self-image would be like looking at a picture album; the first page might have pictures of you at work, the next might depict you with your family and friends, the next might show you involved in sports, then acting as a public speaker... The self-image has many aspects, some of which might be negative, while others are positive. For instance, you might see yourself as a very loving family person but as a frustrated worker, who will probably never be highly successful. However, underlying all these pictures is the way you view yourself as a person. If you view yourself as capable and confident, then chances are that most of the significant areas of your life will be positive and comfortable.

We are actually talking about two very similar yet subtly different concepts: self-image and self-esteem. Your self-image is made up of internal pictures of you doing things: working, loving, playing, learning, and succeeding, etc. Your self-esteem, on the other hand, is your underlying feelings of worthiness. In a sense, the self-esteem gives shape and direction to your self-image. If you feel you are worthy and deserving, you will usually see yourself as succeeding and doing well. Another way of understanding self-image is to view it as an internal-guid-ance system, like an automatic pilot on an airplane. It keeps the plane flying at a certain altitude, a specific speed, and in a single direction. After programming it for those things, the pilot can release active control of the plane, and the automatic pilot will take over and keep the plane on course. If the plane veers a few degrees, up or down or side to side, the automatic pilot steers it back to the intended course.

Your self-image works in much the same fashion. It is programmed by beliefs, thoughts, and attitudes that you have about yourself, and if those parts are structured around a heading for success and happiness, your self-image (like an automatic pilot) will steer you in that direction. If you drift off course, it will take over and get you back in the right direction.

On the other hand, if you have been programmed with negative or limiting thoughts and beliefs, it will direct you toward that path. It will steer you there, even if you consciously don't want it to. You see, the self-image is indifferent as to where it takes you. It doesn't make value judgments or evaluations, or reason its way toward anything. Just as the automatic pilot of an airplane doesn't. It's more like a computer program. It doesn't stop and question why you programmed it a certain way. It just accepts whatever information you give it, and then acts on it. It will take you anywhere you program it to go. You think that an automatic pilot on a plane would dodge a high mountain? Well, it wouldn't. Not if the mountain was on the path for which it had been programmed to follow. It would fly itself and the aircraft right into the mountain. Your self-image works the same way.

The beliefs and thoughts that make up *its* programming direct your course, whether it's a happy one or a sad one. Luckily, you can learn to exert complete control of the programming. You and you alone have the power to exert 100 percent control over the internal pictures and images that you have about yourself.

At any time, you are free to change or modify your beliefs about yourself. When you do this, you change the programming of the self-image. So, even if you have the worst self-image that ever existed, you don't have to keep it. You can change the programming, just like an automatic pilot on an airplane can be changed by the pilot, at any time. I don't mean to imply that changing and restructuring the beliefs and thoughts of your self-image is as easy as snapping your fingers, or pushing a few buttons on a panel, because it does require some persistence and work. There is no getting around that, and you can't do it overnight.

You can begin a little bit at a time, and the effort you put into it can create a lasting and very significant change for the rest of your life. The key to understanding how and why your self-image is so influential in determining your life rests in understanding the power and force that our deeply held thoughts and beliefs exert over us. You might be surprised to discover that virtually everything about your life is a reflection of your belief system. The famous psychologist William James said that belief creates the actual fact. This principle is not new. People from many different ages have realized that it is not external factors that govern us; rather, it is our own self-generated notions concerning the kind of person we perceive ourselves to be.

Marcus Aurelius, an Emperor of ancient Rome, said that our life is what our thoughts make it. Disraeli said that to nurture your mind with great thoughts is to believe in the heroic, which makes us heroes. More recently, Supreme Court justice Cardozo commented that we are what we believe we are. Many have a very difficult time believing this concept. Thoughts and beliefs, after all, aren't objects you can hold in your hand— something you can examine to discover its flaws. When someone is trying to fix a car, for example, the problem can be traced to a physical cause: a folded carburetor, a short-circuit in the electrical system, or whatever. Regardless of what the problem is, it can be seen in physical, concrete terms. It's not subjective; it's not open to debate. If a headlight is out, you can physically see that it doesn't work. There is no dispute.

The idea that thoughts and beliefs actually govern your life, however, is a little more abstract. You can't feel them or touch them or measure them in a laboratory. How can something you can't even see or touch make all that much difference one way or the other?

This is precisely what they do though, and the sooner you realize this, the more quickly you can take the necessary measures to ensure that you are filling your mind with the perception that will attract what you want. You see, when you believe something very deeply, certain forces are set in motion that will create the condition or situation represented by the belief. For example, I know a person who was absolutely terrified of public speaking. He believed that he just couldn't give a speech without being nervous, having his knees shake, and stumbling through it. He was afraid that every time he got up he would forget what he wanted to say, and then freeze. Then he was led through visualizations, where he saw himself giving speeches to large audiences. Doing this, while keeping relaxed, helped this man to change his self-image. He was led to believe that he could give excellent speeches and deliver them well, after being conditioned before the speech. He gave excellent presentations to sizable audiences in his company, even though nothing had changed except his belief about himself.

When the old negative belief had been removed, and a positive alternative was implanted, the man was able to perform admirably. There was no physical change, only an internal one. The only difference was in how he thought and what he believed about himself as a public speaker. Medical science is just now beginning to understand the power that thoughts and beliefs have over our physical health. Most doctors are very quick to concur that the healthiest people are those who have good self-images, and who are not beset with continual barrages of negative thoughts. Research indicates that prolonged worries and mental stresses actually cause the brain to overproduce certain chemicals, which in turn can lead to a multitude of health problems. There is even an entire branch of medicine, called psychosomatic medicine, that centres on the mind-body link with health and wellness.

Many are familiar with what doctors refer to as the "placebo effect". A placebo is an inert or neutral substance given to a patient who is not responding to a traditional therapy. The patient is conditioned, by being told that he or she is going to receive a powerful new drug that will surely work, and the patient is then given the placebo, which is nothing more than (usually) a capsule filled with sugar. More often than not, this works, and the person gets better. The capsule of powdered sugar didn't do anything to help. It was the person's belief about it that did the trick.

Let me tell you a true story, showing just how powerful beliefs can be in affecting physical condition. It is a startling story, and should stand as a very dramatic reminder. A man accidentally locked himself inside a refrigerator box car. Try as I'm sure he did, he could not get out, and he recorded his progress by writing on the inside of the car. The first entry indicated that he was slowly getting colder and colder. He said that there was nothing he could do but wait. He undoubtedly banged on the side, and shouted for help, but there was nobody to hear him. Then, finally, he wrote, "I am slowly freezing to death.

These may be my last words." And they were. The next day, the man was found dead on the floor of the boxcar. He had died because he thought and believed he was freezing. After all, he was in a refrigerated car—a refrigerated car that is supposed to be very cold. Well, under normal circumstances, one would be, but this car didn't work. The refrigerating unit was out of order, the temperature in the car was 57 degrees, and there was plenty of air. The man had died of his own self-created illusion.

Well, this example is certainly a dramatic one. It shows the potential power that beliefs and thoughts can exert in our physical lives. Luckily, for most people, the process is a little more subtle. Beliefs and thoughts create feelings and expectations of happiness or sadness, success or failure, and based on those perceptions, a person is either spurred towards success and accomplishment or bogged down by accepting failure or mediocrity. Your life will unfold according to how you think; what you attract is exactly what you'll get. Like Solomon said in the Bible, as a man thinks in his heart, so is he. If you cannot exert control over your thoughts—how and what you think about—you and your world will have little hope of dramatically altering your self-image.

Chapter 2
Setting Free Your Inner Power

Have you ever felt happy or sad for no apparent reason? Have you ever face a difficult task or trying circumstance, and then been overcome with a feeling that you just could not succeed? Have you ever talked yourself into feeling happy or excited or confident, but had those feelings slip away from you? A friend of mine was relating to me just such an incident, not about himself but about his teenage son. His son had just tumbled onto a rolling discovery. He woke up one morning and suddenly realized that there are girls out there, and unexpectedly, hanging out with the guys wasn't as great as approaching those girls. Well, he wanted to take a girl out on a date, and I'm sure any of you who may have had teenage sons can identify with what I am referring to. A few days went by, and he couldn't quite get the nerve up to ask a girl out. A few weeks went by, and he still didn't have a date. So, he realized that if he was ever going to get a date, he was probably going to have to ask somebody.

His father offered wise council. He said, "Look, just pick up the phone and call somebody."

"What if she says no?"

"Son ... what if she does? Call someone else."

They parried back and forth like this for a little while. The father was trying to reassure the son, telling him that there's no need to worry about being turned down. "Everyone is turned down for a date, or refused something else, at some point. It is part of life. It's no big deal. Beside there's probably a girl just sitting there right now, wishing you will call. Just pick up the phone and call, and you'll see how easy it is." Meanwhile, his son was thinking, and saying, "No girl will probably ever go out with me. I couldn't bear it if she turned me down."

So, on and on it went, but after a while, the father finally got through to him. His son quit vehemently insisting that this girl would surely turn him down, and even if she did, he began thinking that it probably wouldn't be all that bad. So, he began softly replying to his father's reassurances, "You really think so? Well, okay. I'll call her. Who cares if she turns me down or not. I will call someone else, if she does." With his father's help, he was building his confidence. He was flooding his mind with a multitude of positive assertions, and in turn, began to block out the negative things he had been telling himself.

Finally, for the grand finale, bristling with newfound but short-lived confidence in himself, he picked up the phone and dialed the girl's number. At least, he dialed the first five numbers, but before he finished dialing, he was once again swept up with trepidation and lost his confidence, placing the receiver back down. He had talked himself out of having a negative outlook, and gathered his confidence, but just when he was on the verge of putting the positive ideas and beliefs to work, the old negative ones came roaring back with all the suddenness and force of a thunderstorm.

His new ideas, the very beliefs he wanted and desired, got rained on and blown away. Why? Well, the reason is simple: My friend's son had such a difficult time asking for a date, because he had a negative self-image. In his mind, he saw himself being rejected, because his negative self-image was locked within the subconscious mind. Effort on a strictly conscious level, to alter what was in the subconscious, does little good. This is the reason that you feel bad or you feel down sometimes, and have no idea why. You can experience the negative perceptions as seemingly spontaneous feeling. Rest assured, they aren't. Any negative feelings or emotions or perceptions are coming directly from the subconscious mind, and the self-image that's locked therein.

Now, this being the case, why would anyone ever think badly of him or herself? As a person's thoughts and perceptions determine their behaviour and experience, why in the world would anyone purposefully have a negative one? Well, the answer (of course) is that no one does it on purpose. People, in fact, don't really exert very much control at all, one way one the other, over their self-image. Self-esteem is usually formed as sort of an unorganized outgrowth of experience and environment. It is like a boulder rolling down a hillside. The boulder must go downhill. It doesn't stop to consider how and why or which way. Like water, it just takes the path of least resistance—the easiest one available. So, too, does the development of self-image.

Everybody has one, which has to develop. People don't usually stop to consider how or why or which direction it's taking. They blindly stumble along, believing almost anything that seems to be handy, whether it's valid or not. They follow the path of least resistance, contrary to what many believe. You are not born thinking either ill or well of yourself. You acquire your self-image from birth onward. It is generated and sustained by internal evaluations about you and your life. Anytime you make some kind of value judgment concerning your performance or ability or worthiness, you're contributing to your self-image.

For instance, have you ever done really well at some task, and told yourself, "Wow! What a great job I did! I'm really a successful person." Or have you not done so well on occasion, and said to yourself, "I really messed that up. I knew it wouldn't turn out. What a failure I am!"

Well, consequently, you either feel bad or good about yourself.

You generate images of success or failure. Ideas or statements reflecting your worthiness or lack thereof. You don't even have to put these into words. They can be thoughts or feelings, and vague or subtle beliefs or opinions at that. Just the feeling or thought is enough to help you form deep-seated values and judgments. As you gain new experiences, and interact with other people, you tend to reinforce these perceptions, until finally they become habits of thought, rooted deeply in the subconscious mind. Through repetition, all emotions, thoughts, and feelings shape the self-image. There's nothing mysterious or hard to understand about this process. It's easy and it's simple. Your self-image is formed and sustained by the way you evaluate yourself.

As you're probably aware, your mind consists of two major components: the conscious and subconscious. Although both are integral parts of your consciousness, they don't necessarily always work together hand-in-hand. The ideas and beliefs in the subconscious, for instance, can sometimes be completely different from those in your conscious. This is usually the case when someone suffers from low self-esteem or a negative self-image. Negative ideas in the subconscious mind frustrate the positive desires of the conscious mind. Often the person is totally unaware of any limiting ideas locked in their subconscious mind. The individual feels negative, but doesn't understand why. There is no conscious perception of a negative belief; therefore, he or she will conclude that the feeling is just somehow spontaneously occurring. At such times, the person may associate the negative feeling with an event, causing him or her to conclude that "this made me feel bad," but the feeling didn't come from the event. It always comes from the evaluations in the unconscious mind.

The trick is to get the conscious and the subconscious working together. Use your conscious desires, with the beliefs and ideas clustered around your self-image. To understand the process and how to control it, we need to consider how each component of your mind works. As you'll discover, each component is unique, as is what it does to function and how it affects your life. The conscious portion is the reasoning part of your consciousness. It houses logic. You use it to solve problems and reason your way through any number of different things. It allows you to analyze information and argue your way through to some logical and reasonable conclusion, but it has little lasting influence over your self-image. Unlike the conscious mind, the subconscious is not logical. You can't always depend on it to reason its way through two plus two and come up with four. It might startle you with its conclusion. What do you want the answer to be? That might be its response, or it might conclude that two plus two equals twenty-two.

You see the subconscious mind is often quite literal, and it just doesn't think quite the same way that the conscious mind does. Instead of reasoning and arguing and analyzing, it merrily accepts things, often very literally. The subconscious doesn't really care about how logical or illogical, real or unreal, something is. It doesn't let facts get in the way. Like a little child, it will accept whatever you tell it. You don't deserve to be rich, because your wife's brother failed in business and times are bad. The subconscious will be influenced by the idea, and possibly sabotage you, so that you don't become wealthy. It's not going to stop and ask, "Now, what does your wife's brother have to do with your being rich?"

There are several ways the subconscious will accept and cling to a belief, all of which required time, thought (not necessarily conscious), and energy. It basically developed based on the outlook, self-talk, personal experiences, and the experiences of others vicariously shared with you, as well as influences from significant people.

The energy or force that impresses any lessons, learned through any of these avenues, is emotion. These value judgments begin at a very early age, when you're quite impressionable, and then they continue throughout life. A young child is told by a parent, "You're a bad boy (or girl). You broke the window. You shouldn't have done it. What's the matter with you? Can't you behave? You are bad. You never do anything right..." If the child is told negative statements such as these very often, he or she may begin to accept them. The child may actually start believing that he or she is bad and worthless. The idea or the belief will then solidify in the child's mind, and form the foundation of his or her self-image and self-esteem. By the time they reach school age, youngsters have been receiving negative ideas from all sorts of sources, from movies and television, from parents, from relatives and friends, from peers, radio and newspapers, and just about everyone in their environment. Note some of the put-downs and critical name-calling that goes on during the formative, impressionable years: fatso, beanpole, buzzard beak, four eyes, ugly, dumb-dumb, dunce, gross, uncoordinated, stupid, motor mouth, mullet head, sloppy, lazy, and on and on and on.

Being called names such as these can cause the youngster to reinforce any negative ideas and beliefs he or she might already have, even if the names are said in jest. Teachers and other authority figures can contribute powerfully to negative self-esteem through criticism and put-downs. This may not be intended, but sarcastic, critical comments about a person will not usually be just casually accepted. The person may pretend that they're not affected by it, but when a teacher says to a student, "You failed again. When are you going to get your act together? What's the matter with you?" this does more harm than good. That teacher might never realize that he was reinforcing feelings of failure and worthlessness in that young person's mind, the damage from which may take months of positive reinforcement to correct.

When I was in school in the Caribbean, our cricket coach publicly criticized a young lad who was trying out for the team. The coach wanted to see if this boy could handle sharply hit grounders at a close range to the batsman. So, the coach told him to go out to the mid-off position, and field some ground balls from the batting crease. The coach then began to pound several ground balls at the boy. He sure tried to field the balls. Several missed his hand and bounced into his chest. He missed some others altogether. Finally, the coach loudly said that it was the most awkward performance he'd ever seen. "You looked like some kind of an animal out there!" Everybody who heard it laughed. Well, I know most coaches today aren't this way. In fact, I've known many who were masters at motivating young people and helping them to develop self-confidence. Most coaches are selfless in their service and work with young people, but the coach in the example above probably didn't realize what he was doing to the young boy trying out for his team. He walked off that field and never returned again.

Can you imagine the thoughts that must have been racing through this young mind, after that coach's public, biting remarks, and the laughter of all the other boys? "What a failure I must be. I just can't do anything right." Any feelings of low self-esteem or negative self-image that he might have already had were very strongly reinforced. Once we've accepted some basic beliefs and opinions about ourselves, we tend to look for whatever will reinforce that on a daily basis. So, if (for example) you're looking for a better job, and you don't really feel deserving and confident, you might be telling yourself, *I probably will never get this job, either. Many other people have applied, and I am sure they're much more qualified than I am.*

These words, in turn, trigger feelings, and you picture yourself failing. In your mind's eye, you picture yourself being rejected. You accept failure as true for you. Before you even apply for the job, the deck is stacked against you. It makes little difference how qualified and competent you are. You probably wouldn't be hired in a million years, because you're convinced you shouldn't be. You don't think you deserve it, because you see yourself as inferior and lacking. Then, when you don't get the job, what do you tell yourself? *Well, this just proves I'm right. I am really a failure.* Your experience validates and reinforces your negative self-image.

Everyone's life is created and decorated by his or her beliefs. Remember what William James said: Beliefs creates the actual fact. It becomes a vicious circle, which may seem almost impossible to break out of. You *can* break free of any negative thinking and beliefs you have. You *can* break free from them, because you and you alone are responsible. You can exert 100 percent control over every thought and belief you have. Now, this doesn't mean that you do. It only means that you *can*, if you choose to. Every thought and belief you have is a choice. No one has the power to make you believe anything. People can present you with ideas and concepts, but it's up to you to accept or reject them. Would you consider Winston Churchill a confident person? Well, as a young child of 14, he was told he was a dunce, he was slow. he just couldn't do well, and so on. But even though he was told these things by authority figures, Churchill refused to accept them. Just because someone told him these things, didn't make them true. So, he rejected them, and chose to believe in his potential and ability.

As a child, Albert Einstein was described as slow and withdrawn. When his father asked Einstein's teacher what profession his son should pursue, the teacher said, "Well, it doesn't really matter. He'll never make a success of anything." If what other people tell us really make this much difference, then a comment such as this one should've taken its toll on young Albert Einstein, but it didn't. Einstein ignored it. So, what others tell us doesn't always matter. It's what we tell ourselves. How we talk to ourselves in our own mind will determine our self-images. Most people tell themselves lots of negative things. Not even the eventful things and circumstances in your life can make you think badly about yourself. If you fail at something, if you're not doing well in some areas of your life, and if whatever it is hasn't worked out, you don't have to conclude that you are bad, worthless, or a miserable failure. You just don't. You can interpret the event any way you want.

According to statistics, many millionaires suffer severe financial setbacks or even go completely broke several times before hitting on success. What if they failed once and then concluded, that was it? "Well, I guess I can't succeed." I know of a young woman who was a track star in college. Her specialty was the hundred-yard dash. She was so fast that she remained undefeated in her freshman and sophomore years at college. In her junior year, she became the one to beat. She did not disappoint anyone. She took off where she left off, winning her first three meets, but the fourth meet, she ran into some difficulty. Although the competition really wasn't all that tough, and she was (of course) heavily favoured to win, she lost. She didn't even place in the top three. But did she conclude she had failed? Did she begin to doubt herself? Not all. She said, "Well, I was a little off today. I'll do better next time."

You will undoubtedly encounter criticism and self-doubt in life. What you do with it is entirely up to you. Most people fall prey to it. but everyone always has a choice. People are free to evaluate themselves anyway they want. They are free to reject or accept what others tell them.

Once you realize this, you can begin exerting some control over your thinking. There is a cliché in the computer business that goes like this: Garbage in, garbage out. If you program the computer with faulty or incorrect data, it cannot complete a program successfully. In your mind, it is no different. If you feed your mind with negative and limiting beliefs, judgment, ideas, and perception, it will act accordingly, Once you begin to change the program, and start eliminating the negative and emphasizing the positive, you will begin moving in a positive direction. Before you can change your self-image, you really need to know what you're changing. You need to be aware of what your present self-image is before you can expect to change it, and replace the negative aspect with positive ones.

"Know thyself" was the advice given to each person who entered the ancient Greek temple at Delphi. The ancient Greeks realized that self-improvement begins with a careful introspection. Unless you crystallize the thoughts, ideas, and beliefs that you have about yourself, you will find it much more difficult (if not impossible) to really get them under control. There's more to this than you might think. Henry David Thoreau once said that it is as hard to see oneself as it is to look backward without turning around. It really means that people are reluctant to look candidly and honestly at themselves. That's exactly what you must do. Unless you admit any problems or dissatisfactions that you might currently have with your self-image, how are you ever going to change it? The answer is that you've got to be honest, forthright, and accurate in looking at yourself. This is absolutely vital in order to begin changing and leading the life you want.

I want to lead you through a very short activity, where you will be evaluating your current self-image. In your mind, I want you to describe yourself, making a mental list of your traits. It should include both the positive and negative. Mark Twain said that everyone is a moon and has a dark side, which he never shows to anybody. =

It's important to look into that dark side, as well as the other one. You need to be as accurate and as objective as possible. To get started, ask yourself, what kind of person am I? What are my strengths and what are my weaknesses? You might consider some other categories, as you relate to each of these questions: social, occupational, family, education, physical, spiritual, financial, romantic, and recreational. Here are a few additional questions that you might ask yourself. Am I happy right now? Am I attractive? Am I excited about life? Am I confident? Do I believe I am in control of my life? Do I have confidence and hope for the future? How would you describe yourself to someone else?

Now, take a few moments to complete your mental description. By now, you have come up with a skeleton for a story that some magazines like *Reader's Digest* will buy. You could poten-tially even make some money with it, although that sounds a little far-fetched. Well, I really didn't pose that question with the intention of motivating you to work the sketch you just wrote of yourself into a marketable story. But I did have a spe-cific reason in mind. When I suggested that you could write a story and sell it, what was your immediate reaction? Did you tell yourself that sounds interesting, and that it could be a good idea, or did you say, "Well I'm not a writer, but if I were, I could sure give it some thought," or did you tell yourself, "Are you kidding me? I could never do that. Who will want to read about me? Besides, I could never write a story that good anyway. Nobody would ever read it."

Well, whatever it was you told yourself should offer you some basic insight into your self-image. A negative and limited view of yourself would be reflected in statements like "I'm boring. I could never be that good. What a crazy idea." On the other hand, a positive sense of self would be reflected in statements like "Interesting. Sounds like it could be a good idea. If I tried, I'm and sure I will have a great chance of doing it."

Here's what I want you to do. I want you to examine the mental inventory of yourself and your self-image for any nega-tive statements, ideas, and beliefs. Take responsibility for those statements, and realize that you and you alone have made the choice, somewhere along the line, to believe those things about yourself. Then consider the alternative. Must you persist in believing you can't be happy, you can't be confident, you can't be successful, or whatever? Do you have to think ill of yourself? Absolutely not. You can begin right now to reverse that. Begin by affirming to yourself, "I am taking responsibility for my thoughts and beliefs right now. I can become anything I believe I can. I allow only positive thoughts into my mind from this time forth." Of course, this and this alone will probably not solve the problem, but it will help. It will get you started in the right direction.

I trust that the information shared in these pages have shown precisely how you can completely change your thinking. The first step is to understand how important your beliefs and thoughts are, and realizing how you can control them. This is half the battle. Once you've done this, there's just no way you can fail to adapt the kind of self-image you want.

Chapter 3
Investing in Your-Self

You've already leap over the biggest hurdle in building and developing a positive self-image. Getting started, you've learned what self-image really is, you see how it developed, and you've taken active steps to begin adopting a completely positive one. I am continuing this journey by considering one of the most fundamental parts of a positive self-image: self-esteem. As I'm sure you know by now, self-image and self-esteem are very closely linked. You really can't even separate them, any more than you could take a chapter out of a book and expect the book to still make sense. If a major element is neglected, the whole self-image suffers. So, before you can really expect to reap the rewards of a positive self-image, you must be sure that all parts are well-written.

If you wanted to split hairs, you could look at it this way: Your self-image is the image that you have of yourself performing certain tasks and relating to other people. You see yourself, perhaps, as a loving family person, a good worker, a sensitive friend, a talented musician, a versatile athlete, and so on. Your self-esteem, on the other hand, is the underlying feeling of worthiness or value that you have about yourself. Are you a deserving person? Do you feel inferior? Do you feel rejected? Do you think that other people are intrinsically better than you are? The answers to any of these questions will reflect your inner-sense of self-esteem or self-worth. Without positive feelings of self-esteem, you'll be constantly bailing water out of a sinking boat. You may have talent and abilities in many areas, and know that you do, but unless you feel deserving and worthy as a person, these talents will do you little good.

You might look at it this way: Suppose you're shipwrecked on an island; you have the very best radio that science has ever made. With it, you can easily call for help and be rescued in a matter of hours. All you have to do is to lift the microphone from the receiver, depress the switch, and radio for assistance, but alas, the radio is dead. It isn't working. You quickly examine it, and discover that there are no batteries. You forgot them. So, there you are on a small deserted island, with the best portable radio in existence, and you can't even use it. Self-esteem works just like this. Positive self-esteem is the battery that gives power to your life. It allows your potentials and desires to follow a natural course of fulfillment and development, but any strongly held negative beliefs about inferiority or unworthiness will constantly frustrate and block your progress. You won't get what you want, because you have a deep-seated feeling that you don't deserve it. You will never get what you don't think you deserve, or put another way, you'll always get exactly what you deserve. You're always free to choose what you deserve and want. Although you feel non-deserving, lacking, and inferior today, that doesn't mean you must feel that way tomorrow. At any time, you can change. You've just got to decide that you want to. Let me ask you a couple questions: Whom do you love the most? Whom do you admire the most? A friend, a parent, a spouse, or a public figure? Who are these people you look up to? Well, most people probably won't give the answer I'm looking for. The answer I am looking for might surprise you, because it might seem egotistical. The person you should really strive to love and feel good about the most is yourself. You would do well to love yourself, at least as much as you love and care for any other person or thing. Even the Bible says to love your neighbour as you love yourself. Of course, the Bible is not promoting egotism or self-centredness. Many people would be embarrassed to admit they loved or thought highly of themselves, but if you have high self-esteem, you will automatically love yourself, and this enables you to love others more, and receive more love and rewards.

As we continue, you will see why this is true. I hope you're not misunderstanding what I'm saying, which is not hard to do with a sensitive topic like this. When I say to love yourself, I'm not even remotely hinting that you grab a saltbox, stand on it with a strong PA system, and ask everybody to gather around and listen while you loudly proclaim that you love yourself, and are the greatest thing that ever lived. I am not talking about being a braggart or an egomaniac or anything like that. What I am referring to is a quiet inner-sense of complete acceptance, regarding who and what you are. People who stroll about in loud braggadocio, boasting and carrying on about themselves are usually still fighting their own internal battles of insecurity and self-worth. Unfortunately, most of us have been conditioned by family, friends, and society in general to not think very highly of ourselves. Notice how we're talked to by almost everyone: Don't put yourself first; don't think about yourself all the time; other people are more important than you are.

While statements like these are genuinely intended to help, more often than not, they do more harm than good. When we talk to others like this, over and over again, we not only tend to believe the statements but take it one step further, accepting them and jumping to the conclusion that we must somehow be inferior. After all, others are more important, and it's bad to think of yourself first. Therefore, as individuals, we must be less valuable than other people.

Now all of this may not be going on as a conscious perception; most often, it's not. These evaluations occur at the subconscious level, and usually the person isn't even aware of them, but the results are the same: lowered self-esteem. Like every other aspect of your self-image, self-esteem is dependent upon how you view yourself, not on what you actually are. What you are has nothing to do with it. Let me ask you some questions: Do you think that a Nobel prize-winning doctor should have high self-esteem? What about a teacher, or a carpenter? What about a school dropout? Do they all have value as human beings?

Think about your answers for just a moment. Now, if you found yourself grading each of these people's worth or value, on what did you base that rating? Do you feel the dropout is less worthy because of dropping out? Do you think that doctors are worthy people because of what they do?

If you found yourself giving a rating of worthiness like this, where did you get those ideas? What are you basing it on? Who is responsible for your rating system? Is it written on some golden tablets handed down to you from someone up above, demanding that you use it to rate your self-esteem? Of course not. You thought of your own system for determining self-worth. You're the one who said this or that person has a lot of self-worth, because of certain traits, or little self-worth based on the lack of those traits. More importantly—much more importantly—you do the same thing to yourself. Don't you tend to rate yourself by your own notions of what's good and what's bad? *Well, I really did well that time. I'm pretty good.* (Or conversely) *What a failure! I messed up again. I can't ever seem to do anything right.*

Can't you just picture talking to yourself like this? Well look, can't you change your system of rating self-esteem? Of course, you can. If you change the way you talk to yourself, and rate your value, you'll change the way you feel. From the belief comes the feeling and the action. Now, doesn't it make sense to take a good hard look at the beliefs that you have about yourself, and change the ones that are causing problems?

As we continue, you'll be doing just this. You'll be discovering how easy it is to develop a completely positive self-worth, and the way to do so is so obvious you probably wonder why you haven't done it before now. I don't want to get ahead of myself, as there is still more foundation to be laid, but before we start a new house, let's do some introspection. I want to lead you through a short activity that will help you crystallize exactly how you view yourself, right now.

Perhaps you only have vague notions about yourself. Many people fit into this category, simply because they've never really taken any time to analyze themselves. Many people tell me, "Well, I just don't feel very good. I can't always put my finger on it, but there's some kind of a nagging unrest or something, which stops me from feeling confident, giving me feelings of inferiority."

This activity will help you define these feelings. It will help you to focus on any problems of low self-esteem that you might have (whether blatant or subtle), and it's really going to be quite easy. I'm going to ask you to read the following state-ments, and all you have to do is respond to them by either agreeing or disagreeing. Be sure to answer the way you truly feel—not the way you think you should answer.

I don't feel that I'm a very important or likeable person.

I don't see much reason for other people to like me.

Other people don't seem to pay much attention to me, and I really don't blame them.

I don't like new things. I prefer sticking to known and proven ground.

I don't really hold much hope for the future.

I really don't expect very much of myself.

I think I'm unattractive.

Others think I'm unattractive.

Things probably won't turn out right for me.

I'm less likeable than I wish I were.

These ten statements obviously represent low self-esteem. How many of them did you agree with? All right. Let's turn the coin over now, and respond to some that represent a good sense of self-worth. Just as you did before, either agree or disagree.

I'm at least as good as others with the same experience background and training.

Most people I know regard me with respect and consideration.

I have a good insight and understanding regarding life and the person that I am.

I am knowledgeable and accept my weaknesses and limitations.

I really enjoy new and challenging tasks, and I know that I will do well at them.

I don't mind taking risks.

I always expect to do well.

I enjoy being alone occasionally.

I am a loving and unique person just the way I am right now.

I respect other people.

Which group did you find yourself agreeing with the most? Did you find yourself qualifying some of those statements, like I respect *some* other people?

Any of the first set of questions that you strongly agreed with will point to areas that might need some special work. This exercise, of course, wasn't intended to be the last say in the matter, but rather a resource for you to use in gaining insight into how you feel about yourself. The more you know about yourself, the more effectively you will be able to create and internalize the positive self-image that you want. Just like all the other aspects of your self-image, people are not born with low self-esteem; nor do they inherit it genetically from parents or anyone else. It's acquired in several different ways, all of them relating to people propagandizing themselves in a persistent and negative manner, either consciously or subconsciously.

Next, I want to show you how this process occurs, and more importantly, how you can avoid it. I'll cover several of these mental traps as we go along. One way that people talk themselves into feelings of low self-worth is by accepting the opinions and beliefs of others. I'm not referring to physical, political, or scientific opinions and beliefs (although even these opinions can cause some problems, if they're given or accepted in the wrong way), like "I think China is too far away" or "I believe that NASA should start a cattle ranch in outer space." The opinions and beliefs that I'm referring to are those that place a value on you as a person. They're the ones that lead you to view yourself negatively, like "You messed up again. You really can't get your act together, can you? You let me down again. You're just not the person others can depend on. That was a stupid thing to do." When people talk to you like this, and you believe it, you begin to internalize feelings of low self-worth.

Even a seemingly innocent belief, like whether or not NASA should put a cattle ranch in space, can cause problems. Here's how that works. You would first think that this statement could have no effect on yourself, but it can still be turned around to make a judgment about you as a person. Someone can tell you, "Aha! You scoundrel, you don't think that NASA should go to Mars! What's the matter with you? Are you crazy? Are you ignorant? Are you uninformed and backward?"

You see what's happening. People are rating your self-worth based on what you think, what you do, or what you say, any time they make comments or imply any of these types of things to you. This is really not a problem, *unless* you accept their judgments as true. If you tell yourself, either consciously or subconsciously, that this respected authority thinks I'm a louse, therefore, I must be one," you're agreeing with their pronouncement of you, and conclude that you must not be good. The result? Low self-esteem. This is especially likely if you value the person making the statement. If he or she is a significant person in your life, such as a parent, a teacher, a boss, a famous scientist, an authority figure, a family member, or a doctor. Most people swallow other people's the opinions and judgments of themselves hook line and sinker. It's easy to do.

Many a fisher-person wished fishes were this easy to catch. To avoid this, you must be like one of those crafty, old-timer trouts who have evaded hooks and lures all of its life. Don't go for the bait, just because it is dangling in front of you. You have to snap at it. You don't have to accept the negative judgments and opinions of others. You don't have to believe them. Not when it comes to what you believe about yourself. You are the one in charge. Now, here's what I want you to begin doing any time someone offers highly judgmental, biting criticism that reflects on your value as a person: I want you to affirm to yourself that this is only his or her opinion, and say, "I refused to accept it. Just because this person said it is so, that doesn't actually make it so. Then focus your attention on some of your accomplishments; concentrate on the positive instead of the negative.

If the criticism was offered because of something you did badly or even failed at, affirm to yourself, "So what? I'm not perfect; I'll do better next time." Realize that you and you alone are responsible for your feelings and self-worth, and no one can make you feel inferior or unworthy unless you allow it. Later, I'll be showing you in even more detail how and why this is true. You will learn that self-esteem isn't something people have to earn. Everyone has it. You'll see how the dropout I mentioned earlier has as much inherent worth as anyone else. More importantly, you will learn that there is never any reason to put yourself down. You'll learn how to stop doing that, and how to begin feeling good about yourself.

I am now continuing our discussion of self-esteem by asking you to complete three sentences, with whatever first comes to your mind: (1) I am a worthy person, because... (2) I'm an unworthy person, because... (3) Mark Twain's real name was... Okay, I'm only kidding with that last one, but don't forget it, because I want to use it later. Now look at or consider at your answers. Here's how one person answered the first one: I am a deserving person, because I have a loving family, a good job, and a promising future. How does your response compare with that one? Look at the second question, and compare yours with this remark: I'm unworthy, because I got divorced, lost my job, and almost went bankrupt. Sounds pretty grim, doesn't it? How does your response sound in comparison? If you're like many of the people I work with right now, you're probably still evaluating your answers, and this is perhaps the biggest reason that many people have problems with self-esteem in the first place.

They form their sense of self-worth based on some judgment or evaluation that they've made about themselves. As you will be learning as we go along, those evaluations have nothing to do with adopting a healthy self-esteem. Rather, any analysis that you make regarding your self- worth, based on performance, circumstances, or experiences, will just get in your way.

Now, let's look at that first statement, about being a worthy person. There are many answers, but only one that will lead to high self-esteem, and here it is: *I'm a worthy person, because I believe I am.* Yes, you are worthy and deserving person not because of anything you have or did but simply because you believe it about yourself. You don't make yourself worthy and deserving because of doing anything. You could sit in a cave and eat peanuts all your life, and you'd be as worthy as the next person. You may not contribute as much to society. You may not be as fulfilled and happy as others, but you would have as much intrinsic value as anyone else.

Picture two shovels leaning against a wall in the garage. Now close your eyes and visualize yourself selecting one of those shovels, taking it outside and digging a hole somewhere. Now, which shovel is the most valuable? Which has the most worth? You see what I'm getting at: Both shovels have as much worth as the other. One might be used to dig a hole, while the other rests lazily in a shady garage, but that doesn't make it any less valuable. *That's kind of a crazy analogy,* you might be thinking. Well, may be so, but the point is that you and every other human being who ever lived are more like those shovels than you might think at first.

People have value and worth because they exist, not because of what they do while they exist. Obviously, some people accomplish more than others. Some people accomplish great things, while others don't ever do much of anything. No matter what you or anyone else does or doesn't do when the lights are out, when the shouting is over, each person still has innate self-worth.

You have self-worth in light of what you do, not because of it. This brings me to the second stage. Many of you, who have read carefully from the beginning, can probably guess what's coming next (and if you can't, how does that make you feel about your self-worth?): If I am an unworthy person, it is because I choose to *think* of myself as being unworthy. That is the only reason, in the entire universe, that will make you or anyone unworthy. Nothing makes you inferior, unless you allow it. In the words of Eleanor Roosevelt, 'No one can make you feel inferior without your consent.' Every thought you have is a choice. If someone were to read through these pages, that's probably what they would pick up on. I repeated it often enough, and I did so because it's an important concept—perhaps the single-most important concept in the entire chapter. You are responsible. You can change any notion of self-esteem you might have, unless you *choose* to leave it unchanged.

You may have been heavily influenced by others from the past, but now you know you can change. So, let's get a little more specific. Problems with self-esteem develop because people form all kinds of irrational conclusions about themselves, based on their behaviour, in living their lives. The conclusions usually have no basis in reality. They don't rely on fact. Nevertheless, low self-esteem is generated because people convince themselves that these evaluations are true.

For instance, a housewife may feel inferior because she never sought a career in business. She might think she's worthless. *I never got a good job. I've been here in this house for years. I'm just not as good as other women. I feel terrible.* But what does a career, or lack thereof, have to do with a person's worthiness? Self-worth has no bearing on work or lack of it. What about a college student who fails a class? Does this make the person a complete failure, and somehow worthless? Of course not. Failing a class only makes a person a poor student; it doesn't translate into a bad or an unworthy person. The problem isn't with being a good or a bad student. The problem is thinking that grades make one either good or bad.

People tend to rate their worthiness in just this fashion. They analyze how they're doing in areas of their lives that are significant to them, and then they form their conclusions about their worthiness based on their evaluation. As long as you're absolutely perfect, then rating yourself like this would not pose much of a problem. If you always performed well, then you never have any reason to think poorly of yourself. But that's kind of unrealistic, isn't it? Who is perfect? Who doesn't make mistakes? Who doesn't perform badly, at least sometimes? This is where the problem comes in. As long as you're convinced that any aspect of your behaviour or appearance reflects your worthiness, you'll be in deep water as far self-esteem is concerned. But merely rating worthiness based on performance is not enough for some people. They carry the process one step further. They escalate it. When they mess up in any one area, for some reason, they completely forget about any good qualities they have. The one thing they've done poorly somehow negates every good thing they've ever done.

A single bad habit or lone negative traits somehow makes them a completely worthless person. Is this logical? Let me ask you a question: What would you do if your roof leaked? That's right. If your roof leaked, what would you do? Would you fix it, or conclude that the leaky roof made the entire house completely worthless? Well, obviously, you'd repair it. A leaky roof doesn't mean the whole house is worthless. It only means that the roof needs some work. But when people fail at something, or feel they possess some undesirable trait, don't they jump to the conclusion that they are inferior and worthless? Isn't this the way they treat themselves? You bet, they do. Stop rating yourself. It is self-defeating. Analyze your progress and make any course correction necessary. But don't rate your worthiness based on it. You are not your behaviour. You are not your successes or failures. You are a person who does some things well and some things not so well. Separate your behaviour from your work. One does not equal the other.

Remember earlier, when I asked you what Mark Twain's real name was? Does it make any difference what his real name was? Well, it sure did to a friend of mine's daughter. Her seventh-grade English class was studying a section on American literature. Mark Twain, of course, has a very prominent place among the greats of American literature. One question on her test asked what Mark Twain's real name was, and she was supposed to fill in the blank. She was the only person in her class who missed the question. She felt terrible—miserable. Of course, unlike adults, young seventh-grade kids are sometimes overly sensitive to what other people say about them. You will never catch an adult acting that way. She got teased as being stupid by her peers, and she felt pretty worthless about it.

Now, from our far-removed perspective, this might sound a little ridiculous. From where we are sitting, we can clearly see that this test had no bearing whatsoever on a little girl's worthiness. We can perhaps even laugh about it, but I guarantee you, she didn't laugh. She felt genuinely inferior, because she missed the question that everyone else got right. She had based her feelings of worthiness on her performance. Isn't this exactly what we do when we find ourselves with low self-esteem? Instead of saying, "Well, I really didn't do very well; I'll have to try harder next time," don't we tend to overstate the issue? "I failed again. How horrible! Others are laughing at me, and think I'm stupid. How embarrassing. This must mean I'm worthless." Can you begin to see how your performance (or grade or whatever) really has no bearing on your self-worth? Do you know what Mark Twain's real name was? If you don't, do you feel badly about it? Can you see that how what you know or do just doesn't really make any difference to your self-esteem? It's your belief about your actions that contribute to low self-esteem. If you rate yourself as being worthless or inferior and believe it, you will feel and act that way. Do you think you can stop rating yourself and accept your imperfections, with the resolve and determination that you'll try harder next time?

Chapter 4
Inventing Your New Winning Self-image

Abraham Lincoln said that a man is just about as happy as he makes up his mind to be. Lincoln knew that our deepest thoughts govern our lives. He realized that happiness is more an inner-sense of knowing who we are and accepting ourselves than it is of having some physical thing. The degree to which we've internalized a positive self-image, and high self-esteem, will (to a very large extent) determine if we find happiness and fulfillment. If your internal pictures and images are positive, if you see yourself as a loving and deserving person, you will have a happy and fulfilled life. This is the law of the universe and cannot and will not fail. We've taken some giant steps in this direction so far, but there is still some important groundwork to break through.

I will continue our discussion by considering some specific steps that you can take to begin reaping the rewards of a positive self-image. Previously, I have concentrated primarily on removing blocks and negative ideas. Here, I will forge ahead by concentrating on the positive traits that will form your self-image. Let me ask you a question: If you're going to build a house, what would you do first? Would you just start building and hope everything turned out okay? When I was young, I built a rabbit cage following that formula. It was an aesthetic blunder. To its credit, it did hold rabbits, but not for very long, because my parents made me tear it down and start over again. If you're going to build something, and have it turn out right, you must work from a set of plans or blueprints. The same is true of building your self-image. Just wistfully wishing and hoping for a positive self-image will not get you very far. You've got to know what it is that you want before you ever get it. So, with this in mind, let me spend some time helping you determine the characteristics and traits you desire to make a part of your self-image.

The first thing I suggest you to do is think about a person you admire very much. Now, form an image of that person you admire in your mind, and concentrate on why you admire him or her. Look for character traits such as confidence, assertiveness, honesty, dependability, and dedication, etc. These traits are probably the ones you're trying to develop. Now, close your eyes, taking deep breaths and letting them out slowly, and then, as you feel yourself becoming relaxed and at ease, in your mind's eye, look at your own life—look for some evidence showing that how you already have some or even many (if not most) of these traits to some degree. It doesn't have to be in a dramatic way, but possibly a subtle, gentle one. Search for even the smallest clue showing how you've exhibited these traits, at least once. All right, the point that I want you to see is that, in most cases, developing a positive self-image doesn't necessarily mean that you will be adopting a completely new and different trait or characteristic. In most cases, you will simply be nurturing and strengthening what you already have, and what you strongly desire. You will be focusing on what you want and taking active steps to see that you get it. Instead of letting the self-image you desire just rest lazily in the shade, you will be taking it out into the sunshine. Open your eyes and become completely alert.

Now, I want you to concentrate on an ideal self-image. Again, do your best to remain relaxed and open to new thoughts. If you could have any self-image you wanted, what would it be? Do some brainstorming. What are the characteristics of the very highest self-image you can imagine for yourself? Don't allow any limitations to intrude. Don't say I could never do that or I would like this. Just imagine that you are creating yourself according to *your* image of perfection. Imagine you're in a make-believe land, and you can be whatever you want to be. Look at the traits that you noted earlier, the ones you admire in someone else. Which ones do you want for yourself? As you think of the traits you want to develop, form each one into a simple sentence, phrasing the trait as though you already had it. Like this: I am happy. I am loving. I am healthy. I am successful. I am confident. I am loving. I am considerate and patient. I have talents. I feel good about myself. I am intelligent. I'm in control of my life...

I strongly suggest you write down the elements of your ideal image, and write each one with a simple, direct, and positive statement. Jot it down on a clean sheet of paper. "I have a positive self-image." Then, beneath that, sketch the elements of the ideal self-image you would like to develop. Writing down the information is important, because the act of writing causes your mind to focus on it. Consequently, the concepts are strongly reinforced. If it's convenient for you to do so, write down your ideal self-image. At this point, you may either write out your self-image or formulate it in your own thoughts.

When you're ready to proceed, you should have either formulated thoughts of some specific traits, or have written it down. These will form a blueprint for you to follow. What you have right now is only a rough draft, and like most blueprints, you're going to have to work with them a little, to be sure that everything fits together correctly. So, let's take a look at what you've written, or your thoughts of what you have, and determine if it needs some improvement. To start, search your list and make sure there are no negative statements. For instance, if you've said or written, "I won't be jealous," or "I don't want to treat people impatiently," cross them out right now. Any statement containing negative language (don't, won't, can't, shouldn't, etc.) will work against you. This is very important. If you want to form a self-image based on what you *don't* want, rather than what you positively desire, you going to end up frustrating your progress. This is because a statement like, "I won't be inconsiderate," actually causes the subconscious mind to concentrate on the wrong thing. Instead of focusing in a positive way on being considerate. It zeros in on being inconsiderate. You have probably experienced this principle before or know someone who has.

Imagine a brand-new waitress in a restaurant carrying a large tray of food. She's awkwardly trying to balance it in one hand, and has to use her other hand to place the plates of food on the table. The restaurant is crowded, and she has to dance her way through the crowd with the tray of food carefully balanced in her grasp. In a circus, she would be a sensation with such an act. In a restaurant, she's just another waitress. Anyway, she's concentrating on arriving at that table with all the foods still on the tray, and someone yells, "Hey watch out! Don't drop that tray!"

If she listens to this, concentrating on it, what you think she's likely to do? Well, first of all, she will probably form an instant image in her mind of dropping the tray, and secondly will tell herself, *I sure hope I don't drop it.* If she continues concentrating on this long enough, chances are she'll either drop that tray or another one, sending food, drink, and dishes spilling all over the place. The negative "don't" statement plants the seeds, which eventually causes the action to occur. The statements you make concerning your self-image work exactly the same way. If they state what you don't want to do, you're going to be in for stormy weather.

The subconscious will usually zero in on the negative action and push you toward it. If you tell yourself, *I won't drop this tray,* you'll end up with broken dishes, spilled food, and unhappy customers, not to mention, a less-than-pleased employer.

Here's something else to consider, when evaluating statements: even subtle wording matters. "I hope to become more confident." Do you think that this effectively conveys a message of confidence? Well, not really, because it plants seeds of doubt. The word "hope" suggest that you would like to be more confident, but you're not very confident that you will. So, the subconscious remains unconvinced. You've given it a very weak argument, and it's not sure if it should instill feelings and beliefs of confidence, or if those words it's simply wishful thinking. After all, you're not really sure yourself. You only hope. You're not adamant and insistent.

Examine all the statements you've thought of and written down concerning your ideal self image, and get rid of the ones that express any sort of doubt or negative action. Cross them out. Don't toss them, rewrite them, or rethink them. Structure each one in a simple sentence that is clearly expressive of the image that you want, as though you already have it.

Here's an example: "I am patient." This simple and to-the-point sentence states, in no uncertain terms, that you are a patient person. There's no misunderstanding. Structure each aspect of your ideal image in just that way. I am patient. I'm successful. I'm fulfilled and happy. With sentences like these, lay out whatever else you want to be a part of your self-image. At first you may balk at this. *How can I write or say that I'm patient now, when I know all-too well that I'm not? It's sort of like lying to myself.*

Is it? Well, is it? Remember earlier, when I had you examine your life for even the very smallest incident showing that you already possess most of the traits you are trying to develop?

Perhaps you may presently be impatient more often than not. That's not the point. The point is that you already *are* patient (or whatever), to some degree at least, on some occasions. Do not lie to yourself. You aren't claiming you have something that you don't. What you are doing is focusing on the trait. You're causing your subconscious mind to begin accepting, and consequently reacting, in a more patient, accepting manner. Once your subconscious does this, the dominoes have been lined up and tripped. The effect will ripple from your consciousness outward into your physical experience. As you believe internally, so shall you be externally. That's a principle that's been repeated from the beginning.

Suppose, though, that you're different from most people. Suppose you possessed not even the smallest bit of the trait that you desire to adopt. Should you still write, "I am a patient person"? You bet you should. You might remember, from earlier chapters, that the subconscious cannot distinguish reality from fantasy. If you convincingly tell the subconscious something, it will believe it. In believing it, the subconscious accepts the idea, and then goes about validating it. In validating it, your life mirrors the belief in your physical actions. You become the trait or characteristic you convince yourself you are. All lasting and significant changes begin internally. It then flows outward and is reinforced through physical action. Shakespeare put it this way: "Assume a virtue if you have it not." I'll have more to say about that as we continue. As you work on your self-image, another important thing to keep in mind is to always use the present tense. Don't say, "I *will* be a kind, loving person." Write, "I *am* a kind, loving person." This is important, because the subconscious is very literal. If you focus on the future tense, using the verbs "will or shall", the subconscious takes you at your word. It will assume you want to be kind and loving not now but sometime tomorrow, and when is tomorrow going to arrive? Never. Tomorrow is always in the future. So, if each day you say, "I *will* be kind and loving," the literal subconscious assumes you don't want it now. The result is that it will make little effort to propel you toward becoming whatever it is you told yourself. "I am a kind and loving person, today. Right now." This makes the subconscious realize you mean business. It sets in motion the forces necessary to begin propelling you toward your goal. You may think I'm splitting hairs, but I'm not. I'm giving you tried and proven techniques that produce the quickest possible results.

I am sure there are many different ways that you can initiate sweeping change in your life, but most of them require a lot of time and effort. I'm giving you shortcuts. Why wander around, if you can get where you want to go quickly, easily, and safely? These techniques will do that for you. Just be sure you follow them carefully. Now, let's put all this information together and organize your self-image into simple present-tense, positive statements. This will be just like rewriting the rough draft of a story or a news article, to recap what you need to do.

Use only positive language, and avoid all negative statements, and statements that express doubt. Use only the present tense. Structure the sentence to express the fact that you already have the image now.

Now, once again, I want you to think about your ideal self-image. Get a clean sheet of paper, and at the top, write "my positive self-image". Below that, write affirmations reflecting the image you want. Be careful to phrase them correctly. If you need to, you can go back and review how to do this. I also want you to use a separate sentence for each aspect of your self-image. For instance, if you have three or four or nine or ten traits that you desire to develop, use a different sentence for each one. For example, I am a loving person. I am a successful person. I am a healthy person. I am a happy person. This will help you to focus on each individual aspect. When you focus and concentrate your attention on it, you energize the affirmation. This helps the subconscious to much more readily and quickly accept each one. You're going to be using this blueprint in several different ways.

Later, put some thought into it. Write your-self image. This will be the final draft for now. If you're not writing it out at this time, spend a few moments concentrating on your ideal self-image. Form each aspect of it into a separate statement, following all the guidelines that we just covered. Now that you formulated your highest ideals for your self-image, what are you going to do with them? Well, first of all, you now have a master plan. This is what you are going to become. Secondly, you'll be using the statements almost all the time, from now on. Thirdly, you will plan some actions based on them.

I want you to read each statement aloud. Put as much positive emotion behind it as you can muster. You'll be making positive affirmations, much in the same fashion as the ones you've already stated. Out loud, say, "I am a completely confident person." "I am filled with patience." "I am a happy and successful person." Make your statements like that. Use emotion. Really get into it, and feel it, because emotion is the force that convinces the subconscious. It causes the subconscious to stand up and take note of what you're telling it, over and over again with feeling. It makes it accept the ideas and beliefs. I also want you to make a list of the affirmations and carry the list around with you for a few days, and when you have some idle time, get it out and read the statements. If you're in a crowded location, where reading aloud might disturb others, then simply repeat it in your mind, being careful to emotionalize them as you silently rehearse the affirmation.

After a short while, you will probably be able to repeat all of them from memory. There's nothing wrong with this. I encourage you to do it, but to begin also spend some time looking at the written statements. Seeing them in writing, concentrating on the words, and enthusiastically affirming the new beliefs, will all help to reinforce them. If the above is practised for twenty-one days, your self-image will improve, and there will be noticeable differences in your behaviour and manner.

Chapter 5
Achieving Excellence

Seek neither perfection nor excellence
for you will not grow; seek only improvement
for you will learn, grow and change each day
Princess Etherline Joyette (1920-1985)

In a play, actors must learn their lines and act their part. The first step is to become acquainted with the script. A lot of time is spent memorizing it, and getting the dialogue down just right. At first, the conversation and stage presence seem a little awkward. This is understandable, because actors are attempting to portray other characters, to assume traits and characteristics that they may not normally possess. But as the cast practices, time and time again, an amazing transformation begins to take place. The actors begin to move around on the stage as if it were their own home or their own backyard. They begin talking and acting as if they really were whoever they are portraying. If an actor becomes deeply involved with the character, he or she may even take on some of those traits in real life.

In real life, I am reminded of Mario Lanza, who portrayed the great Caruso in a movie in the early 1950s in London. He became so involved that he took on some of Caruso's mannerisms in real life. Leonard Nimoy, who played Spock in the science-fiction series *Star Trek,* also mentioned that, at least at one point in his career, he became so wrapped up in the character he was portraying that he would sometimes find himself acting a little like Spock in real life. Well, what has all this got to do with self-image? Everything. In the previous chapter, you determined a detailed description of your highest, most ideal self-image, and you performed some positive programming exercises to begin putting those beliefs to work for you.

This chapter is going to take the process one step further, and will begin by putting this new image into practice in your life.

In your life, combining physical action with the positive programming of the subconscious will be the most effective and fastest way to strengthen and reinforce your new beliefs about yourself. Harvard psychologist William James, said that, if you wish to possess the qualification or emotion, act as if you already have it. Shakespeare, you might recall from the previous chapter, told us to assume a virtue, if you have it not. In plain language, James and Shakespeare are telling us this: If you want to be assertive, act assertively. If you want to be patient, confident, and happy, act those ways, and you'll become them. After all, the world's a stage, and we are merely actors playing out our role.

Once you've given this principle an honest effort, you'll see how easy it is to begin acting and becoming exactly what you desire to be. Sometimes when I mention this to people, they treat it somewhat skeptically, saying, "I can't start controlling my temper," one man told me.

"Why?" I asked. (Can you guess what he said?)

"Because I've been this way for a lot of years. You can't expect me to change now."

Well, we've already talked about disbelief in some detail earlier. You learned that you can change. There's no such thing as "I can't start acting this way or that way, because I was born differently." Could you imagine if the director told an actor to act patiently, and the actor said, "I can't do that. I've never been patient my whole life. This sound ridiculous, because a person can *act* that way, even if it doesn't seem to come naturally to them.

Dr. George Weinberg based an entire book on self-creation. On this very principle, says Weinberg, every time you act, you add strength to the motivating idea behind what you've done. He elaborates on this, explaining that every time you do something, the motivating idea or feeling that prompted you to do it is intensified. It can be an idea about yourself, others, the world... Whatever it is, it's reinforced when you act on it.

Now, here's what I want you to do. Refer back to the positive image that you determine for yourself in the previous chapter. Look at it. Examine the traits and characteristics that you are becoming, and ask yourself this question: In what ways can I begin putting into practice my new image? What can I do to begin practising this new behaviour? You're looking for opportunities to practice what you've been preaching to yourself.

After you've identified several, give yourself an assignment. Write it out. Outline specifically how, when, and where you can begin practising your new trait. If, for example, you are becoming more charismatic and warm towards others, identify a specific situation in which you can act this way. After you've identified it, write out an objective. It might look like this: "When I'm talking to others this afternoon, I exude warmth and friendliness in my voice and mannerisms. I radiate genuine concern and charisma." Writing out specific assignments gives you something concrete to work with. A detailed task to carry out is a good way to begin validating your progress. Let me make it a little more clear. Say, for instance, you're attempting to become more assertive. You've written the affirmations. "I am assertive and confident. I assert myself with ease and pleasure. This is natural and easy for me." Secondly, you've done the relaxation sessions, and have programmed these ideas into your subconscious.

Now, all that remains is for you to go out and be assertive somewhere. So, here's what you do: Review your normal daily routine in your mind, and find a situation where you could assert yourself. It doesn't have to be some big major event; a trifling one is fine. At first, you might be more comfortable looking for some minor way in which you could assert yourself. Maybe it's something as simple as helping to decide where to eat lunch with your friend. So, you get a piece of paper and write down, "Tomorrow during lunch, I suggest exactly where I'd like to go." The next day, when it's time for lunch, make yourself carry through with your intent. Don't sit passively in the backseat, saying, "Oh, I really don't care where we go. Where everyone goes is okay with me." Sit up and make your views known. Tell your friends, "I'd really like to try this new café. Let's go there."

When you're home for the evening, set some time aside to evaluate your progress. Get out the written objective, and determine if you really followed through with it. A word of caution here though. You're not at all interested in how well you performed. *It makes no difference.* It doesn't matter if you are successful in swaying your friends to have lunch where you wanted to go or not. It makes no difference if you stumbled through the incident. It makes no difference if you felt timid shy, weak, ineffectual, or whatever. Even if you broke out in a sweat and felt faint, don't worry about it. The only thing that matters, and the only concern you should have is whether or not you initiated a new behaviour. As long as you persist, each attempt becomes easier and easier. If you almost passed out with fright the first time you attempt a new behaviour, the next time you want practice-perfect. Rome wasn't built in a few hours. Although I wasn't there to watch it being built, I can safely say it took a little longer.

Concentrate on the effort, not the result. Results will follow, in the form of positive feelings and actions. It might not be instantaneous, but sooner or later, they will come. As you master small occasions with your new behaviour, gradually work yourself up to larger and larger ones. Make a point to challenge yourself—to make it easy to bite into the assignments. If you are trying to improve your weight-lifting, what challenge would there be by beginning with the one-hundred-pound barbell and continuing with it every time? By not increasing the weight when your strength improves, you will be winning the battles but you'd lose the war. Your game wouldn't improve. It improves largely through the excitement of taking new risks, improving your strength and become a little more skilled each time. The point is to steadily progress, choosing to act out your new behaviour in bigger and grander ways.

What you are doing, of course, is breaking old habits and learning new ones. Whatever your self-image is now, it's only there because you've taught yourself (either knowingly or unknowingly) to act that way. If you have some lingering uncertainties about how you developed the self-image you now have, I strongly suggest that you go back and review the first few pages of this book, because they deal specifically with how and where your self-image came from. As you're probably aware, old habits are sometimes difficult to break, especially if they're deeply ingrained in the subconscious. Relaxation sessions and physical actions are extremely effective in loosening the grip the subconscious may have on your self-image. Before that grip is loosened, you should be aware that, unless you are an unusual person, you will probably experience some awkwardness and discomfort as you attempt to change. The new behaviour may seem unnatural; it may not seem or feel exactly right. Psychologists call this cognitive dissonance.

Cognitive dissonance refers to the fact that a person learns new behaviours in two-ways: intellectually and emotionally. First of all, you intellectually know what you want. You may be desiring to be more assertive or patient, for example, so you listen to lectures on the subject, perhaps also reading books and acquainting yourself with how to develop the new behaviour ... but that's only one step. That's purely intellectual. Learning the new behaviour emotionally is the next step, and this one usually takes a little longer and may require a little more effort. You must break any old emotions connected with the old ways of acting, and learn the new ones associated with the behaviour or the trait that you desire. The lag time between the intellectual acceptance and feeling the appropriate emotional reaction is the cognitive dissonance, and this is precisely where the well-intended but faint-hearted often get drawn off target. They want the new self-image, diligently learn how to do it, but grow faint-hearted and discouraged, because the new behaviour doesn't feel right.

"This is just not *me!*" one exasperated lady told me.

"If it's not you, then who is it?" I asked. "You mean you're someone else?"

"Well," she said, "the new behaviour doesn't feel right."

"Of course, it doesn't," I said, "because it's brand-new. Not only are the old habits still there at first, but your subconscious has yet to learn how the new one is supposed to feel."

Think back to when you first learned to drive a standard-transmission car. Before you ever got behind the wheel with the keys in your hand, someone had to show you how to do it. You learned where each gear was, when to push in and let out the clutch, depress the accelerator, how far to push the clutch in, and how to let it out. Intellectually, you knew how to drive the car. But what happen when you actually did it? The car probably lurched back and forth like a dying dragon. I still remember trying to go to the store for my girlfriend's mother when I was a young lad. I had never driven a standard transmission before, but of course, I was too proud to admit it. She told me to take her car, and so I did. The noise from those gears grinding against one another sounded more like the charge of the light brigade, and surely annoyed the automobile. I really felt embarrassed, but the transmission survived, the car survived, and after a few days of practice, I became a little better at it. Before long, I was driving around with graceful ease, shifting gears without even having to think about it, because the action had become a habit. My subconscious had taken over.

Adopting your new self-image is no different. What you're learning is different, but the process isn't at all. When you begin attempting your new behaviours, gears may grind a little, and you might feel awkward and self-conscious, but don't give up. Don't generalize away such feelings, concluding, "I tried this, but it was so awkward, I know I could never do it." That's a faulty assumption. What if you'd given up on driving a car just because you have a little trouble the first few times? We'd still be walking today, not because you didn't know how to shift gears, but because you decided that you could never master it. Learning any new skill starts out challenging and uncomfortable, and then becomes easier and easier, eventually becoming a habit. Developing your new self-image is no different. You'll come to a point where you no longer even have to think about the new behaviour. You won't have to consciously even try. The new behaviour will become habit. It will flow naturally and easily from you.

You even may look back on your old habits and tell yourself, "I used to be like that. Oh, come on... I *couldn't* have been like that! With that kind of behaviour? It wouldn't even *feel* right. It's not me!"

Touché. Here are several things that you can do to soften any discomfort you might experience as you begin to act out your new self-image. Each relates to detachment—trying to avoid becoming too emotionally involved with how well you're doing. Strive to separate your performance from your effort. I touched on this a little earlier, and I know it's easier said than done. After all, it is difficult to remain steadfast when you break out in a sweat and your tongue is stuck to the roof of your mouth. But you can do it.

First of all, realize that difficult doesn't mean impossible. Happiness and fulfillment are often built on overcoming challenges. Look upon adopting your new self-image as a fun challenge. Focus on the rewards, outline the pale, and constantly remind yourself how much better and rewarding your life will be after you've accomplished your goal. Write these things down. Think and dream about them. This helps focus your attention on where you're going, instead of worrying about how you're going to get there. It keeps your vision on the forest and off the tree.

Secondly, as you begin acting and behaving differently, make affirmations silently in your mind. We all talk to ourselves constantly. Sometimes, when you are doing something new and different, you might say something like this to yourself: "I feel really strange trying this. What if I fail? What if others see me flopping about like a fish out of water? What if they laugh at me? It just doesn't feel right. I wonder if I should go through with it."

When you feel these kinds of thoughts encroaching, stop then immediately.

A bottle filled with fresh-squeezed orange juice can't also be filled with sour milk. It is either one or the other. Nor can your mind have two opposite thoughts simultaneously. Don't let the sour milk spoil your dinner. Concentrate on the positive beliefs in your mind. Scream the words "stop", "cancel" and then make positive assertions about the new behaviour, saying, "I release and dissolve all negative thoughts and ideas. I allow only positive thoughts in my mind. I feel wonderful and good. I love life. This new behaviour is getting easier and easier. It is becoming totally natural."

This brings your attention back to where you want it to focus: on becoming the new person. If you refused to give the old ways energy, by choking off the feelings and thoughts associated with them, they will get weaker, wilt, and will eventually die, like plants out of water. DO IT—even if you have to force yourself. Difficult definitely doesn't mean impossible.

I began these pages by comparing acting out your new self-image with putting on a play. This idea might help you to remain detach and become less emotionally involved. Look at it just this way: In your mind's eye, see yourself as an actor, and this new self-image is your role to act out. Realize that, in the beginning, you may stumble through a few of your lines. You might even make some wrong movements on the stage, but who cares. You're learning a new part. You're rehearsing and getting down your lines and movements. All you need is a little practice. In the comedy *As You Like It,* William Shakespeare wrote that all the world's a stage, and all the men and women are merely actors. They have their exits and their entrances, and one man in his time plays many parts.

Look upon yourself in this light. Be detached. You're an actor. As an actor, choose your part carefully. Write your own scripts. Make them the highest, most ambitious visions of your most wonderful dreams. Then go forth on the stage and play. You'll be amazed at how well you can do. Once you've decided to do this, you'll also discover what most actors and actresses already know. It is fun.

REFLECTION

(1)   In your life, combining physical action with the positive programming of the subconscious will be the most effective and fastest way to strengthen and reinforce your new beliefs about yourself.

(2)   Dr. Weinberg said that every time you act, you add strength to the motivating idea behind what you've done. He elaborates, explaining that every time you do something, the motivating idea or feeling that prompted you to do it is intensified. It can be an idea about yourself, about others, about the world, or whatever, but it is reinforced when you act on it.

Chapter 6
Tapping Your Vast Power Within

Think for a moment that you are on board a spacecraft. You are preparing to leave the ship, and venture into the empty weightlessness of space. This is your first trip away from the earth, and as you get into your spacesuit, you are filled with eager anticipation and excitement. You are asking yourself what will it be like to drift alone through space. How will it feel? From a portal in the capsule, you see the darkness of the universe. It is almost overwhelming. Little pinpricks of light are shining back at you. You have never seen such a tapestry of starlight in your entire life. Waves of awe, joy, and wonder wash over you, again and again, as you fasten your helmet and prepare to take your first step, and venture out into the dark empty void that beckons to you, awaiting your arrival. Anyone who's ever dreamed of spaceflight, or has closely followed the space program, has probably imagined things like this. Such an adventure would be thrilling indeed.

Several years ago, someone asked an astronaut this very question. What was it like to step out of a ship into weightlessness for the first time? For the romantic at heart, the astronaut's answer was less-than dramatic, and downright disappointing. The astronaut explained that, by the time he finally got on with the real space walk, he had already done it so many times in practice that the real thing seemed almost routine. It was old hat by then.

The entire crew had practised for eight weeks in simulators on earth. Each mentally rehearsed the procedures and projected themselves into the actual experience countless times. It almost seemed as though they had been born spacewalking. In training for their mission, the first astronauts used an extremely effective and safe training resource that you too can begin using: visualization.

They practised for an entirely new experience by first visualizing themselves doing it. Years ago, no one had ever walked in space, so there was no one to ask about it. Simulators were built to approximate space-like conditions, and the pilots would practice in the simulators while mentally projecting themselves into the actual experience. In their minds, they weren't just in simulators. They created vivid pictures and feelings, as if they really were in outer space, and by doing this, they gained invaluable experience—experience so real and lifelike that the real thing, by their own admission, seemed almost routine.

I'm showing you how you can use visualization techniques and applications to help enrich your own life. Actually, you're already a pro at visualization. Anytime you have a mental picture about anything, you're visualizing. Since words, thoughts, plans, and dreams all evoked mental images, you're constantly forming these mental projections all the time.

Let's look at a typical example: Suppose you're planning a vacation. As you decide where to go and what to do, what's going on in your mind? You're forming mental pictures, impressions of the place that you intend to visit. For instance, you're planning on hiking through the Grand Canyon, and a friend of yours (who has been there before) starts telling you how big and massive the rock formations are, how green the grass is around the springs, how quickly the wind can come off the cliffs, and how awe-inspiring the towering walls of red rock are. What goes on in your mind as you listen? You tend to see those things that your friend is telling you about. You not only see them but begin projecting an image of yourself being there as well. You see yourself in the Grand Canyon. You see those red rock Cathedrals. You feel the wind blowing through your hair, and feel the warm sunlight against your skin. If you think about it often enough, and vividly enough, it will be almost like being there.

This same technique, which we all used constantly, can be an extremely important resource in helping to internalize your new self-image. You can mentally project yourself into any situation or circumstance, and see yourself behaving and acting exactly the way you want. You can see yourself transformed into the positive self-image that you are striving to develop. Actually, you've already been doing this. You have already been directed to visualize certain conditions, to see yourself already having a positive self-image, and a high sense of self-worth. On this note, I want to more specifically show you how you can develop this skill. I will concentrate on visualization techniques, and show you how they can be used to produce even faster and more dramatic results in adopting your self-image. The techniques do work well. It is indisputable—just ask an astronaut, or if there isn't one handy, ask any athlete or actor, who use visualizations to help improve their lives in many different ways. In a way, visualization is your trump card. In the previous chapter, I spent considerable time showing you how to begin acting out your new self-image. Well, it is a lot easier if you practice in your mind first, as will be illustrated in the guided-relaxation session following this. You practice the same way the astronauts did, by imagine yourself doing the new behaviour well before you ever confront the actual experience.

Visualizations work so well because the subconscious cannot distinguish reality from fantasy. If you strongly imagine something, the subconscious reacts as if it were real. Because of this, properly thought-out and well-developed visualizations can be used to train the subconscious well before you actually experience the new situation. You can carefully instruct it on exactly how you want to react, and how you want to feel. If you practice enough, the real thing will be no different to the subconscious than the practice session. A new trade or behaviour becomes habit of mind first, and then habit of action. Visualizations hasten your progress. I'm now going to show you how to begin using visualizations to reach your self-image goal. First, bring to mind some of your objectives. If you look at the objectives you wrote (or call them to mind), you'll see specific, detailed things that you're trying to accomplish. For instance, one of the behavioural goals you might've written is to assert yourself by asking people to smoke somewhere away from your desk at work. Previously, you felt a little timid and reluctant to take control of your airspace. You finally realize that you have every right in the world to politely ask people to take their cigarettes and cigars elsewhere. You don't like smoke. You don't want to breathe it. You don't want it to burn your eyes. All you're going to exercise is your right. Your new self-image is one of confidence and assertiveness in this matter. After you've written the specific objective, you will then visualize yourself doing what the objective stages specify. Set a few minutes aside to relax, and be still. Create the situation in your mind. See yourself at the office. Picture someone lighting up. Then see yourself politely but firmly telling the person, "I would really appreciate it if you would smoke somewhere else. The smoke really bothers me. Thank you for being considerate." In doing this, see how the person responds in a friendly and warm manner, by apologizing and either moving away or putting the cigarette out.

As you form these pictures in your mind, you need to inject positive emotion into the scene. Effective visualization contains more than just picture. It needs to be used with strong emotion, and confidence in your new behaviour. Sometimes, emotion that occurs spontaneously is an outward growth of the vivid and realistic pictures or concepts that you generate. Occasionally though, you may have to help yourself along a little bit, by stating affirmations just like you did in the visualization. For instance, if you see yourself performing a new behaviour, affirmed yourself. "I feel so good with my new action. Positive energy flows through me. This action is easy and natural for me. It feels so good."

The motion is the energy or force that impresses the seriousness and reality of the visualization on the subconscious. It is the dimension that gets you what you want, and gets it fast. Look at your list of objectives to determine how you can begin using visualizations to accomplish them. Form examples where you can see how easy it will be. You can use it to pattern your own visualizations after that.

From the beginning, I implied that visualizations take the form of mental images and pictures, and so they often do ... but not always (for some individuals). In fact, for some people, they never did. Many people new to these techniques say, "I don't see anything. How are you supposed to do this? I concentrate on what I want to picture, but there's nothing. There was no pictures or images." This is because some people's minds work differently. Some people are visual thinkers and others are conceptual. Those in the latter category tend to feel images, rather than actually see them in crisp pictures. They form ideas and concepts in their minds concerning the event being visualized. They may seldom (or never) actually see the picture, but the ideas and the feelings generated by the event are intense enough that they produce every bit as positive result as those who see pictures or mental movies. A feeling of being there is generated. An impression of reality is created. Consequently, the subconscious is impressed with the visualization and learns the intended lesson. When I use the term "visualization", I use it to mean more than just seeing. It also includes feelings, sensing, knowing, and describing. So, don't be concerned if you can't see picture or situations or movies exactly the way you think you should.

Whether you actually see detailed pictures or merely generate feelings and impressions. What I'm calling visualization will be every bit as effective. There is no single method that everyone has to use. Each person is different, and each will have a slightly different way of doing it. The only things you should do to make it effective is to keep the visualization positive. Make sure it specifically addresses the issue, and be sure to inject as much strong positive emotion into it as you can. Although your visualizations are most effectively when done while in a state of deep relaxation, by no means should you limit them to just this. You can do them any time.

For instance, if you have some spare time at work or at home, you can close your eyes and project yourself into the condition that you are working with. Just see yourself performing the new behaviour in your mind's eye. Here is how easy and fast it can be. Unless you're driving now, or engaged in some other activity, close your eyes right now. Take a deep breath, let it out through your mouth, and relax a little. Now imagine getting up for the day. It is tomorrow, and you are arising out of bed. See yourself happy, and smiling, and all excited about the daily routine. Feel good about yourself. Then you affirm. "I am filled with positive energy. Everything turns out good for me today. I'm excited about this day." Now open your eyes. That's it. That's all there is to it. You've just done a very quick visualization. Little sessions like these are very effective reinforcement. They strengthen new beliefs. New behaviours. This should be looked upon as an adjunct to the exercises that you will do with my guidance later on.

The above exercises are not the primary programming activity, but they are excellent secondary ones, and as you can see, they can be done very quickly and easily, and at almost any time. In some cases, you don't even need to close your eyes. After you become proficient with this, you can do it any time, with your eyes open, and form impressions and images in your mind's eye, even though you might not be concentrating all that much. Even that much effort will help. The most effective visualizations, of course, are those you're doing in a state of deep relaxation, and the reason for this is that, when your body is very still and relaxed, you are working more directly with the subconscious mind. At the end of this chapter, you will be given some exercises that are designed to assist you with deep relaxation and visualization.

As you begin visualizing the behaviour of your new self-image, it's equally important to stop any negative pictures that might flash through your mind from time to time. These negative images result from the old thought habits—the ones that you're changing. They may seem to come spontaneously from nowhere, but they don't. Every image you have is the result of some belief that you had at some time in your life. If you see an image of failure, or you have a feeling of failure, or some other negative occurrence, it springs from some belief that you have buried in your subconscious mind, relating to the relevant condition. It could also be a conscious belief, but more than likely, it comes from some deep-seated feeling in the subconscious.

Consider this example: You're about to go on a job interview. You want this job badly, but you really don't have all that much confidence that you're going to get it. So, as you begin preparing for the interview, you think, *I won't get this job. What if I screw up this interview and fail?*

Well, when you think these thoughts, what mental pictures accompany them? You probably see yourself stumbling through the interview and not getting the job. This is an example of a negative visualization, and you must exert control over these. They impress the subconscious just as much as the positive ones do. If you allow them to continue, then your positive programming is not going to have the effect that you want it to have. You control these the same way you control negative mind-talk or self-talk. When some negative image enters your mind, immediately and forcefully tell yourself, "Stop!" "Cancel!" Then affirm yourself. "I release these images; all negative thoughts and pictures instantly dissolve from my mind. Only positive thoughts and positive energy flow through me."

After doing this, make yourself visualize the very opposite. Picture the positive behaviour—force yourself, if you have to. Make positive affirmations as you form the positive picture. You are provided continual reinforcement to discipline behaviour such as this, and all those negative beliefs you may have. They will weaken the continued effort and you must will dissolve them completely. You'll be surprised that, just a little while down the road, you will be looking back and realize that you don't think negative thoughts as much anymore.

"I don't have those negative pictures popping into my mind! I don't have those feelings of self-doubt or inferiority!"

In conclusion to this point, I want to reaffirm that you can control your thoughts. You can exert control and allow only positive thoughts and pictures to enter your mind. Of course, there must be some effort and persistence. The more you do it, the easier it becomes. That's what is so wonderful about this whole thing. It becomes easier and easier, week after week. You will find that it becomes more and more naturally a part of you. After a while, positive thoughts become habit. They flow from you naturally and easily. You won't have to make any special effort to think about them, any more than you have to stop and think about how to tie your shoelaces.

REFLECTION

(1)   When I use the term visualization, I use it to mean more than just seeing. It also includes feelings, sensing, knowing, and describing. So, don't be concerned if you can't see picture or situations or movies exactly the way you think you should.

Whether you actually see detailed pictures or merely generate feelings and impressions, what I'm calling visualization will be every bit as effective. There is no single method that everyone has to use. Each person is different, and each will have a slightly different way of doing it. The only things you should do to make it effective is to keep the visualization positive. Make sure it specifically addresses the issue, and be sure to inject as much strong positive emotion into it as you can. Although your visualizations are most effectively done while in a state of deep relaxation, by no means should you limit them to just this. You can do them any time.

Chapter 7
Feeling Great

How do you feel about your physical appearance? Have you looked in the mirror this morning? Are you happy with what you see? For many people, physical appearance and attractiveness become major stumbling blocks. What about you? Are you concerned about being attractive? Well, if you are, you're part of a growing crowd. According to a 1985 *Psychology Today* survey, the majority of both men and women professed concern over their appearance. The survey indicated only a scant 18 percent of the men and 7 percent of the women responding to the questions were completely satisfied with how they looked. It also revealed that a negative body image can actually cause problems with self-esteem. People who felt good about their bodies were reported to be healthier, happier, and better adjusted than those who didn't. Obviously, in order to internalize a completely positive self-image and high self-esteem, you must work to feel good about the way you look, in order to be satisfied with your appearance. Unfortunately, far too many people needlessly formed deep-seated negative beliefs concerning their appearance. Usually, such perceptions are far from realistic. In fact, you may be surprised to learn how attractive you are, and how much control you can exert over your physical appearance.

You'll learn that your appearance is little different than other aspects of your self-image. It is almost completely dependent on internal beliefs and ideas that you have about yourself, and you can actually cause physical changes in your appearance by altering any deeply held negative beliefs. In these pages, I will show you how to do this.

First of all, you need to understand that attractiveness (or lack of it) is only a definition of what is attractive to you. It may not be to someone else. For example, let's consider art. What kind of art do you like? Do your friends also like it? Do they find the same beauty in your favourite painting as you do? Let's get a little more specific. What about a famous and widely acclaimed work, by a famous artist such as Rembrandt.

Rembrandt, as you probably know, is generally acknowledged to be one of the greatest artists of all time. On one occasion, I saw several Rembrandt's on display in a museum. Were they beautiful? Well, many of the people viewing them didn't think so. Some thought the paintings were only so-so. Others didn't like them at all. Some people had absolutely no idea who Rembrandt was. The point is that there were many different opinions concerning the beauty of even very famous works of art. Their beauty and their attractiveness were only an opinion. Now who is right and who is wrong? Were the people who thought the paintings were absolute masterpieces correct? Were the ones who wouldn't have them if the museum offered the paintings free of charge right? The answer is that no one was right, and no one was wrong. Each person determines for him or herself what is aesthetically pleasing, and what is not. It is the same process as true physical appearance. It is a definition. You're either attractive or unattractive based on how you choose to think of yourself. Your beliefs determine your physical attractiveness. Your belief is your definition. Change your belief, and you will dramatically change the way you actually look. Now does this sound preposterous? At first, perhaps, but we're not finished yet.

You will see how and why this is true in just a moment. First of all, I want to clarify an important point. There are obviously certain limitations regarding your physical body. These relate to heredity or other physical factors. These are the only aspects of your appearance that you really can't exert much control over. For instance, the colour of your eyes, your height, or skeletal features. What I am referring to, though, are your deepest beliefs about the body you have. I'm stating that how you perceive it will not only determine how you view yourself but also how others react to you. This is far more important than cosmetic surgery or any physically contrived alteration. Because, once you form realistic, positive beliefs about your physical appearance, you will reflect a beauty and comeliness that far outshines and outlasts any external modification.

To begin with, you need to accept what you already have. Comparing appearance to someone else's is a common demon that hunts many people. Some person becomes a role model for them, and they try to look exactly like him or her. Since this is an almost impossible task, they end up getting down on themselves for falling short of their expectation. I implore you to avoid this trap. You'll only end up disappointing yourself. Why would you want to look like someone else? There's no need to do so. You will realize that you have a beauty and attractiveness all your own. Accept what and who you are, and allow your own inherent beauty to shine. Another way people get themselves in trouble is by allowing others to determine their attractiveness. Listen to what some people say: You sure have aged. You're skinny. You're fat. You've got a bad complexion. You've lost some hair. You've lost your figure. You put on weight. On and on they go. Some are even more blunt, and actually tell people they're ugly or unattractive. When I was a teenager, I came home from school one day and found my next-door neighbour crying on her front porch. She was in my class, and we were pretty good friends, so I asked her what was wrong. She said that someone had told her she looked like a witch. It wasn't the first time she had heard that term, and now she was feeling that she really was ugly. But she didn't look like a witch. I comforted and reassured her all I could, but it was a damaging blow to her self-image. It took some time for her to resolve this issue, but she did, going on to become a very happy and successful model. If you allow others to influence you with their opinions, you might end up not wanting to look in a mirror. Don't give into that. Realize that some people just won't think you're attractive. Remember, attractiveness is an opinion, like in judging art. It is a very subjective opinion, and the only opinion that matters concerning your beauty is yours. Be yourself, and be comfortable with yourself.

To begin changing your appearance, you have to get rid of any negative idea that you are unattractive. You could have the most beautiful, striking appearance in the entire universe, and still view yourself as unattractive, if you hold negative beliefs about your appearance. Now, that may sound a little far-fetched, but it isn't. Occasionally, a negative belief will centre around a single feature. The individual discovers some flaw—a mole, a line, a wrinkle, or a pimple. That person then becomes a magician, not just an ordinary magician, though, for an ordinary one wouldn't do. He or she becomes a master magician—a modern-day Merlin. He or she does what no stage magician has ever done. The person fixates on the mole or the pimple or whatever, and it is magically transformed it into Mount Everest. It becomes the single worst catastrophe that ever visited the human race.

Such a blight obviously makes a person just about the ugliest individual who's ever lived. There is nothing much that could be done about it. Well, that sounds a little preposterous, doesn't it? And it always will, to everyone, save the pariah with the mole. That person is convinced that his or her appearance is doomed. There's an easy escape from this type of self-downing. If you should discover something about your appearance that is not readily changeable, don't over-generalize about it. Chances are, you're probably the only one who notices it any way. One flaw or blemish will not negatively affect your appearance in any serious way, unless you allow it to. If you fixate your attention on it, you'll actually draw other people's attention to it. On the other hand, if you forget about it and focus on your positive traits, others will as well.

Being overly self-conscious about any aspect of your appearance will usually lead you into deep water, as far as your self-image is concerned. Worrying about your hair, your clothes, your face, your feet, your ears, etc. creates a negative mental climate, and you already know how a negative mindset gets in the way of what you want. The negative ideas will manifest itself every single time. There's just no escaping this law of life. I remember a salesman friend of mine who turned up at my office one afternoon, behaving rather strangely. He seemed nervous, impatient, and kind of on edge. And finally, I asked him if something was wrong. I thought perhaps he had suffered some trauma or something terrible had happened, based on how he was acting. He had. At least, he *thought* he had.

"So, you notice," he said.

"Noticed what?" was my reply.

Well, it seems my friend had just gotten a haircut, and the barber hadn't cut his hair the way my friend wanted. It was styled a little differently. It was a new look for him, and he wasn't used to it. He thought it made him stand out like a sore thumb. In truth, though, the only thing that made him stand out was his odd behaviour. I hadn't even noticed his hair.

In the same way, any negative fixations you have about your appearance can cause you to draw unwanted attention to it. The irony is that some perceived loss or lessening of the way you look will seldom capture other people's attention. Rather, it's your negative thoughts and beliefs about it that get you into trouble. Your internal beliefs are the real determiners concerning the way you look, in terms of the way others perceive you. There are also a number of physical, external conditions, that you can control. Most of them are pretty obvious. For example, to look your best, be sure to attend to personal hygiene; make really sure that your clothes are clean and your hair neatly fixed, and so forth. Also, if you're interested in appearing normal by society's standards, then you'd want to be sure that you dress in an accepted way. If you went around in a loincloth like Tarzan, people might want to stare at you. If this is your purpose, then of course, such behaviour would be rational and logical. On the other hand, if your self-image is one of a normal citizen, then you might want to save the loincloth for a trip to the jungle, and wear more acceptable attire in your normal routine. The point, of course, is to be sure your clothes reflect the positive person you are.

You'll also normally feel and look better if you get the rest that your body needs. If you receive the right amount of sleep, you'll tend to appear bright-eyed, vibrant, and filled with energy. Each person's sleep needs are different. There isn't some magical quota that you have to have. Just be sure you get enough sleep. Your lifestyle and body needs will determine just how much that is. Diet and exercise are also integrally linked with your physical makeup. If you constantly satiate yourself on rich, fattening foods, and get very little or no exercise, well ... you shouldn't be surprised if you end up with considerable girth. In other words, you'll gain a lot of weight, which you will probably want to avoid if it is something that is of concern to you. If you are consistently experiencing difficulty with your weight, then you might find an exercise program on the subject helpful.

Taking physical measures to modify your appearance, in a positive way, is the first step toward recreating the way you look. The second is to internalize positive beliefs and expectancy, not only directly related to your appearance but also pertaining to every aspect of your self-image and self-esteem. The latter is more important than the former, because if you attach your self-worth in any way to how you look, and you aren't satisfied with what you look like, you're setting yourself up to be miserable. As such, you should take steps to improve your appearance when and where possible, and then get on with life. Don't fixate on your appearance. Be determine to feel good about yourself and be happy. Real beauty is a direct reflection of the kind of person you are. Beauty and good looks begin within, and then flow outward. Your appearance is a statement of how you perceive yourself.

Let me ask you a question, to show you how this works: When is a good-looking person ugly? It might sound like a contradiction. Well, it isn't. I will explain. Have you ever met someone who at first seemed really attractive, but after you got to know them, you changed your mind? Chances are that you've experienced this. A person with attractive physical features can be looked upon with something far-less than enthusiasm, if that person suffers from some negative character trait. If the person is usually quarrelsome or even bitter, if he or she thinks negatively of everything and everyone, or if they are not enjoyable to be around for whatever reason, they will be looked upon as unattractive, regardless of their physical features.

This is because the person's negative beliefs cause others to view even their physical appearance negatively. On the other hand, with a positive self-image and high self-esteem, almost everyone will appreciate a person's beauty and attractiveness, regardless how they look physically. This (as I've said) is because true beauty is far deeper than an image reflected back at you in any mirror. It is a direct reflection of your positive beliefs and outlook on life.

You can also begin to modify your appearance by internalizing positive beliefs about specific aspects of it. For instance, if you want to appear more energetic and more vibrant, you can begin doing so by affirming, "I am filled with positive energy. People see me as a happy, enthusiastic, positive person. I am bright-eyed and energetic." Once you make the affirmation, follow it with the visualization. See yourself as a happy, enthusiastic, positive, and bright-eyed person. If you are trying to tone up your muscles and firm up your body, you would (of course) exercise, and in addition, start visualizing and affirming: "My body is slim and trim. Every muscle is firm and well-toned. I love to exercise, because it helps me look the way I want to look." Working on specific areas like these, with affirmations and visualizations, can really make a noticeable difference. This is because the subconscious mind controls your metabolism, and many of the other internal functions of your body that determine the way you look. That being the case, if you work with the subconscious in this way, you can actually make it manifest physical alterations in your appearance. Obviously, I am not referring to those changes which defy your genetic composition, such as your height, your eye colour, the shape of your head, the number of fingers on your hands, and so on. I'm referring to more subtle changes, such as complexion, fitness, weight, energy level, and overall appearance. These can all be greatly enhanced by the subconscious mind.

To effectively harness your inner-resources and alter your appearance, you should treat it the same way you would any other aspect of your self-image. You follow the techniques and procedures already outlined in this book. To recap, here's what you do:

First, remove negative thoughts and beliefs concerning the problem, using whichever technique I've described that work best for you. Second, establish a goal that will determine how you want to look, and then write objectives reflecting your desire. Third, write down positive affirmations concerning your new desire. Fourth, say the affirmations out loud, with passion and conviction, while visualizing what you want. Fifth, outline any physical action you can take to help you accomplish your purpose, and then follow through and take the action. And sixth, continually reinforce your new beliefs through affirmations and visualization throughout the day.

REFLECTION

(1)   Taking physical measures to modify your appearance in a positive way is the first step toward re-creating the way you look. The second is to internalize positive beliefs and expectancy, not only directly related to your appearance.

(2)   There are obviously certain limitations regarding your physical body. These relate to heredity or other physical factors. These are the only aspects of your appearance that you really can't exert much control over. For instance, the colour of your eyes, your height, or skeletal features. But how you perceive them will not only determine how you view yourself but also how others react to you. This is far more important than cosmetic surgery or any physically contrived alteration. Because, once you form realistic, positive beliefs about your physical appearance, you will reflect a beauty and comeliness that far outshines and outlasts any external modification.

(3)   Don't fixate on your appearance, be determined to feel good about yourself and be happy. Real beauty is a direct reflection of the kind of person you are. Beauty and good looks begin within and then flow outward. Your appearance is a statement of how you perceive yourself.

(4)   You can also begin to modify your appearance by internalizing positive beliefs about specific aspects of it. For instance, if you want to appear more energetic and more vibrant, you can begin doing so by affirming, "I am filled with positive energy. People see me as a happy enthusiastic positive person. I am bright-eyed and energetic." Once you make the affirmation, follow it with the visualization. See yourself as a happy, enthusiastic, positive, and bright-eyed person.

PURPOSE

By
David A. Joyette (1970)

We are all teachers, guides and mentors
To the minds before us.
It is our responsibility to direct these
Minds along right channels.
Ours is the great privilege of seeing
These minds flower and blossom forth.
Ours is the proud burden of developing the
Minds of all, so that they become responsible
citizens of this universe.
Therefore, we are the molders of tomorrow's world.

Chapter 8
Change! Why we must!!!

Although this project is about difficulties with negative self-image and sub-conscious programming that is common to all people, as a black man, I would be remiss if I did not also address a few particular obstacles that the black population face, in regard to racial discrimination, poverty, education, social justice, and the emotional struggles of life. From the beginning of slavery to the 21st. century, race has been the driving force affecting opportunities for people of African descent. The question of whether this has changed presently is ambiguous. America (Canada and the USA) has certainly evolved from a place of slavery and segregation to the self-proclaimed "land of opportunity", offering equal rights and prospects for all. Yet there are still signs of inequality within the social construct of our nation.

If one were to take a look at both countries' work field, they will notice the differences in positions acquired by black people and Caucasians. Blacks usually work at minimum-wage jobs, living paycheque to paycheque, and if they are fortunate enough to acquire an adequate paying job, their employers are generally

Caucasians, who usually own the major businesses and corporations. This inevitable conflict has emerged from both countries' history of unfair and unequal treatment of people of colour. Neither of these societies have completely eradicated the problem with racial discrimination and inequality within the work force, which has created the growing wealth gap.

In America, issues of race and class are tied together like a chain of DNA; one cannot address the issue of class without referring to the demographics of race. The methodology of determining the variations in social class was established in the mid 1960s, and has not changed in nearly fifty years. Within this time span, there have been many studies conducted that reveal the bases of how our society classifies people into social groups, with race being a significant determining factor in their results. Figures suggest that both Canada and the USA have a problem with the connection between race and class, being that the social classes are more segregated than integrated, which evolves from the disproportionate poverty level among people of colour. Reflecting back in time to when there was a Black America, which consisted of "Negros"—poor slaves being mistreated, discriminated against and oppressed because of the colour of their skin—America was socially and physically divided, because of extreme racism, which went on for years until the Civil Rights Movement (USA) in the 1960s, which granted African Americans (no longer Negros) full legal equality, and changed the state of the nation.

In Canada, this came about in 1982, with the Constitutional Charter of Rights and Freedoms, which declared that people of colour were free from discrimination, segregation, marginalization, and inequality, and were given opportunities similar to whites, so they could gain economic and social status within the nation.

As blacks began to prosper in the society, they still faced the struggles of competing with whites, who seemed to always be a step ahead in every social aspect, such as employment, education, and housing. The majority of blacks were constrained to occupying low-wage, minuscule jobs, like housekeeping or maid services, and could not afford proper housing, so they lived in the "slums". Most importantly, they could not afford a full education. Therefore, many blacks were poverty stricken, and labeled as the working poor or "underclass". People were condemned to the double jeopardy of being black and poor.

Our society declares itself to be a nation of equal rights and opportunities, yet the fact is that racism remains, deeply rooted and with no end in sight, and will continue to be cumbersome to deal with in a just society. The unemployment rates, drop-out rates, and homeless rates are still higher among blacks than whites, thus suggesting that blacks are plagued by negative circumstances, or rather, are disproportionately represented on those socioeconomic levels. To show how this is perpetuated across Canada, African Canadian children are being taken into child welfare on dubious grounds, 41 percent of the children in the care of the Children's Aid Society of Toronto were black, when only 8 percent of all Toronto's children are of African descent (according to the *Toronto Star*).

Mathew O. Hunt, Associate Professor of Sociology, doing research on issues of poverty and homelessness, professes that race is the single strongest factor of beliefs about inequalities. His research goal was to prove that most researchers "neglected the issue of race and ethnic differences in socio-psychological processes, in which people assume there is no evidence to suggest that the determinants of beliefs and attitudes should vary across race-ethnic lines." He further pointed out that the historical oppression and continued segregation of blacks is an obvious source of group distinction, in how the beliefs of poverty are shaped.

From the 1960s to the present, there has been little change in the dynamic of the North American workforce. Blacks exhibit shockingly, high unemployment rates compared to any other race or ethnic group. Why is this phenomenon reoccurring today? One could reason that the economy is recovering from a recession, where numerous workers were laid off, businesses were filing bankruptcies, and well-paying, unskilled jobs were disappearing from the market. As such, the work field become increasingly competitive, and individuals have to obtain higher credentials and qualifications, such as university degrees, to earn a good living in today's society.

In a society heavily concentrated on a person's image, regarding your economic and social background, stereotyping, prejudice, and discrimination affects the distribution of power, wealth, and opportunities, which creates the proliferation of inequality based on individual differences. These practices and actions are difficult to change, and is a daunting challenge for any country to address and change, because they are rooted in tradition and cultural beliefs.

Subsequently, another reason for black joblessness is due to economic and political competition for jobs and power, in which acts of prejudice and discrimination become evident. Though it's illegal in America and Canada, a person can still refuse to sell you a house based on your religion, race, or ethnicity. Similarly, employers can reject a fully qualified applicant because of his or her race or ethnicity. They just have to be discreet about it. These misguided behaviours are profoundly overlooked, and go unchallenged for fear of creating hostility or controversy within the society.

Blacks are constantly fighting to outshine other racial groups in education, politics, and jobs, because they are frequently pre-judged and underestimated. Social media has stained and criminalized the image of blacks, by portraying them as uneducated, aimless, and lazy individuals, living in ghettos and dependent on welfare cheques. This form of indirect discrimination and prejudice, in which social media dehumanizes and ridicules people of colour, ultimately affects blacks, making them feel less-than human and inferior to other ethnic minorities.

The gap between white and black unemployment figures are mainly due to a faulty job market, in which blacks are the last to be hired in a good economy, and the first to be released when there is a down turn. An example of this, was described by the *Toronto Star:*

"The unemployment rate for black women is 11 percent, 4 percent higher than the general population, and they earn 37 percent less than white males, and 15 percent less than white women."

Blacks have equal opportunity for obtaining all qualifications, and are expected to receive a high-end job, just as whites are, yet blacks with the same level of education, qualifications, and experience as whites continually have lower employment rates. Many sociologists have studied this issue, and developed conclusions as to why this unevenness occur. Edelman determined that the structural change in the economy, and the changing demographic, accounts for much of the persistent, higher poverty levels among blacks—especially when continued discrimination is added to the equation.

He also stated that there could be something wrong with the structure of the labour market, in which there are too many jobs that do not pay enough to live on, which is a problem hurting people of all races, though it disproportionately impacts people of colour, who have less education and experience continuing discrimination in the labour market. It is therefore predicted that, for people of colour with low income, poor education is a direct cause of the higher poverty rates. The question of why there are disproportionate representations of blacks living in poverty does not produce a simple answer, because reasons are socially constructed, which can be disputed or supported.

The issue of poverty and blacks is solely created by the social construct of North America, which links past dilemmas of segregation and racism to present economic and social issues, which are not easily resolved. There have been countless analyses and studies done to identify and create a policy or statute that affect the practices of systemic racial discrimination, but they lead to nowhere. One can only hope the nations address the issue, realizing that there is a problem that needs to be fixed, and hope for positive results.

According to research, black people are the least successful people in the world. White people are five times richer, yet black people are the most religious, believing that God will miraculously bless them with wealth by their attendance in church. Yes, it is true that white people and racism can be blamed for some of the sufferings that black people face. But not all. Some of these are also self-inflicted.

Why? Because black people refuse to think for themselves. One of the greatest gifts God gave to mankind is the ability to think for themselves, as quoted in the Bible. Just a reminder about the story of the ten talents, as told in Matthew 25:14-30 and Luke 19:11-27. A man gives his servants his goods. He gave five talents to one, two to the second, and one to another. The first two doubled their talents, but the last one buried his; it was, therefore, taken from him and given to the one with the ten talents, and he was cast out of the presence of the Lord. Therefore, despite all the ills we have faced, we must take responsibility for future successes in our lives. We do not have the luxury to passively wait for change to occur. We must think actively and make things happen.

Other cultures have faced racism, segregation, and enslavement, and even persecution and death. The question is this: "How did they overcome these adversities and survive, thrive, and even achieve success beyond the dreams of their oppressors?"

To start, let us look at the Jewish culture, and the Japanese Canadian Internment. According to the first four Books of the Bible (King James version), Jews were enslaved in Egypt, and after their freedom, they became a nomadic people without a country. They travelled throughout Europe and Asia.

Now, just a brief history: During the World War II, Hitler's Germany had occupied almost all of Europe, including Poland and France. When the Soviet Union invaded Germany, Hitler was in the final stage of eliminating the Jewish people, resulting in their persecution and murder in political Europe, including European North Africa, as well. This genocide, The Holocaust, methodically exterminated approximately six million Jews.

Japanese Canadians experienced racial injustice right here in Canada, with the Japanese-Canadian Internment. This was the removal of Japanese Canadians from British Columbia, following the invasion of Hong Kong, the attack on Pearl Harbour, and the Canadian declaration of war on Japan. This forced relocations, and subjected Japanese Canadians to government-forced repatriation to Japan. Japanese Canadians were removed from their homes and businesses and sent to internment camps in the B.C. interior, and to farms and internment camps across the country.

The Canadian government shut down all Japanese-language newspapers, enforced curfews and interrogations, and took possession of businesses and personal property, selling it in order to fund the internment. Some of the items seized were fishing boats, motor vehicles, houses, and personal belongings. Although this was not as horrific as slavery and the Jewish Holocaust, both the Jewish Culture and the Japanese Canadians overcame these ill deeds. Why?

Because they did not sit around and blame Hitler and the Holocaust, or the Canadian Government for every moment they had been oppressed. No, they viewed all their people as one unified, cohesive body, educated themselves, and worked hard to benefit even the country that had wronged them. They looked at life positively, worked hard, and created a trail that others could follow. They looked at adversity as the inspiration to do better, and achieve more, adding value to society and themselves.

On the other hand, if people of colour continue to think of the past, they will continue to live in the past. They will never feel valued, and their efforts will not be truly rewarded. Until we spend the time, take the risk, and make the effort to learn the system(s) of the country we live in, this will not change. There must be a dogged determination to succeed at success. We must know ourselves—our strengths *and* weaknesses—and utilize our strengths to achieve what we want for the betterment of our people and society. We must educate our minds, our will, ourselves, and like-minded people like us—in all aspects of cultural development, knowledge, and philosophy—and use the business model as a guide, exploring plans of action and utilizing all the resources we need to achieve our desired outcome. It is only then that we will overcome the scourges of oppression, deprivation, and poverty. We must remove the shackles of mental poverty and slavery, by changing our way of thinking. Whatever we do, it must benefit all of our peoples, not just you, the individual. "Benefiting you" only perpetuates and fosters the slave mentality, and hinders developmental progress in our culture and our community. We must first look at all our people (family members and alike) as equal members in our society, regardless of what they are. Whether they are straight-haired, dark-skinned, educated, or lazy (or not ambitious), they are valuable, equal, and have a role to play in our growth and development. None of us is better than the other, and therefore, we must adhere to this simple fact: "Each of us wants to succeed, either at success or at failure." If we do this, we will succeed.

The task before us is to logically foster and focus that emotional energy, which drives us to succeed at success and maximize our potential to benefit all.

Let us explore ideas about leadership in the following context: What does it take to be a leader who can excel in the society of the 21st. century? Certainly, it will require leaders who will strive to meet the more complex and intense expectations of our changing world, to focus on the changes and shifts in our current society. The changes we have seen throughout the world have been both simultaneously exciting and traumatic for people in leadership positions. The pace can be frantic, and demands for results, quality, and continual success are relentless. But the rewards are equally abundant for the professionally equipped leader who can meet these challenges.

What is this person? This could be you.

The kind of leader who excels in this environment is one who takes responsibility for results, creates a motivational environment, and develops his people, who in turn, take responsibility for their own performance.

This is an ambitious goal to strive for, but you have the potential to realize it. I trust that, as you read through these pages, you will gain ideas that can help you get there. Our leaders must use their knowledge to bring the black community together, helping individuals to build confidence in themselves and others. If you have no self-confidence, what will you share with others? They must share new vision, seek new ideas and tasks, and ask for participation and assistance in achieving desired goals. We must give our people the autonomy to make decisions, without fear of reprisals or criticism, and they must give reasons for any and all decisions made. These measures will go a long way in building trust and confidence in our people.

Bear in mind that some of us can only criticize, as it is the only thing we know. Why? Because we have been taught to do so by our parents, teachers, peers, and society. This attitude must change, because we are looking for *solutions*. Not problems. Criticism is designed to look for problems. The more we look for problems, the more we will find. The paradox is also true: If our goal is to solve problems, and find solutions, and we *look* for solutions, we will surely find more of them. We are responsible for our lives, our actions, our thinking, and our behaviours. We all have different values, and these are based on the action(s) of our parents and how we were raised in our community and by society. We do not all share the same experiences, have the same knowledge, or cultural heritage, or colour, or religion. Therefore, and we are unique in every way. Just consider the following:

The truth is "You are."
Your Experience is your Reality.

Your Experience of the universe flows
through you.
No one else
Is experiencing what you are experiencing,
Or what you have experienced,
Or what you will experience.

Let us look at the word "responsibility" for a moment; it is made up of two words, "response" and "ability". "Response" means to make an answer; act or behave in answering. "Ability" means the capacity or power to do things. Therefore, responsibility must mean we have the power and capacity to act, behave, and answer for what we do and who we are. This brings us to the concept of responsibility, put forward by Admiral Hyman Rickover, who said: **"Responsibility can only reside in a single individual. You may share it with others, but your share is not diminished. You may delegate it but it is still with you. You may disclaim it but you cannot divest yourself of it."**

If you believe this, you will never look at blame or fault, for these are only debatable in a court of law. We are one hundred percent responsible for what happens in our lives. There may be incidents in our lives for which we are not the cause, and thus should not be blamed; however, we are responsible for how we handle life's situations. We are one hundred percent responsible for our reaction to life's events, and one hundred percent responsible for putting ourselves in a position to experience that event. Therefore, we have the power to find solutions to all of our problems, and not to wallow in self-pity and the ill-conceived notion that "he did it to me, and that is why I am suffering." It is your life. You owe it yourself to act in accordance with all your knowledge and ability to preserve life with dignity, and take responsibility for all of your actions.

Let us explore some of the reasons for *not* staying the course. If it is your way to continue the blame game, then rather than learning from your past, you will make someone else responsible for your life in the present. You may say, "I could be successful, if it had not been for____! They did it to me!" By thinking this way, you willingly relinquish your power, and your responsibility for your past experiences. You have become an effect or result of your past experience. When people blame others for their experience, they often live in the past. They wallow in self-pity and doubt. Is this what you want for future generations? No. Then only you can stop repeating history.

All you can say about the past is that it was exactly the way it was. It does not matter whether the individual liked the experience or not. The past is inflexible, and whether we enjoyed it or not, it is "perfect" for everyone. In this context, each individual's past is unique and complete for that individual; therefore, it was "perfect." We cannot be who we are now with a different past. To move out of this rut of blaming others for our situations in life, we need to ask ourselves, "How can we learn from our past experiences?"

By resisting the past, or feeling badly about it, or making the past "wrong", we will not learn from the experience itself.

Responsible individuals mentally record past experiences, review them, and learn from mistakes and misrepresentations of themselves and others. Reviewing a mistake, or some kind of failure, enables such individuals to alter their thinking and themselves, or circumstances, to be more successful in the future. Let us look at the words of Alexander Pope: "A man should never be ashamed to say he has been wrong, which is but saying, in other words, that he is wiser today than he was yesterday."

Let us look at reasons why we must take responsibility for change: Our greatest enemy, within us, is our attitude or habits of thoughts. We feel we are incapable of living the life we were born to live, and therefore, translate our thoughts into actions—actions that encourage and foster racial and societal forces to work on us from the outside. From the days of our enslavement, many of us bought into the slave mentality. We accepted the white man's pronouncement that we are an inferior race, and even when we came to understand that it was a false pronouncement, it continued to dominate our collective psyches; it was a powerful indoctrination.

The following is an infamous and chilling example of how that mentality was ingrained into our ancestors, and into succeeding generations. As we go through an excerpt from George Fraser's *Success Runs in Our Race*, we will see how the process of indoctrination was done. I will be quoting part of Willie Lynch's speech, from whom the term **lynching** is derived. Lynch was a British slave owner in the West Indies, probably of Jamaican heritage, who used mind-control techniques on his black slaves, and then advocated the use of those manipulative techniques to other slave owners. He was invited to the colony of Virginia, in 1712, to teach his methods to slave owners there, and these are the words he passed down. I think you will find them haunting:

> *"In my bag here, I have a foolproof method for controlling Black Slaves. I guarantee every one of you that if installed correctly, it will control the slaves for at least 300 years. My method is simple and members of your family and any Overseer can use it. I have outlined a number of difference(s) among the slaves; and I take these differences and make them bigger. I use fear, distrust, and envy*

for control purposes. These methods have worked on my modest plantation in the West Indies and [they] will work throughout the South. Take this simple little list of differences, and think about them. On top of my list is "Age" but it is there only because it begins with "A." The second is "Color" or "Shade," there is intelligence, size, sex, size of plantation, attitude of owner, whether the slaves live in the valley, or on a hill, East, West, North, or South, have a fine or coarse hair, or is tall or short. Now that you have a list of differences, I shall give you an outline of action but before that, I shall assure you that distrust is stronger than trust and envy is stronger than adulation, respect and admiration.

"The Black Slave, after receiving this indoctrination, shall carry on and will become self-refueling and self-generating for hundreds of years, maybe thousands.

"Don't forget you must pitch the old black versus the young black and the young black male against the old black male. You must use the dark skin slave versus the light skin slaves and the light skin slaves versus the dark skin slaves. You must also have your white servants and overseers distrust all blacks, but it is necessary that your slaves trust and depend on us. They must love, respect and trust only us.

"Gentlemen, these Kits are keys to control, use them. Have your wives and children use them, never miss an opportunity. My plan is guaranteed

and the good thing about this plan is that if used intensely for one year the slaves themselves will remain perpetually distrustful."

Based on the knowledge of your inner-self, have there been any change(s) in the way you think and act in dealings with family, friends, and society? If the answer is NO, then you must ask yourself why? Because you have continued the **lynching** process by training your children to do and behave the way you feel.

Our men must not mistreat our women, for they are the fulcrum, the nurturers, and the fore-bearers of our society and future generations. You must understand this simple fact: "People respond as treated" and if we do not deal with this, by consciously educating our will and retraining our minds to develop better knowledge skills, positive mental attitudes, and which good behaviours and habits that will take us to higher levels of awareness, our culture will not improve, and we will be doomed as a people. For we will only be qualified for the lowest-paying jobs in society, no matter how many university degrees we have. Our attitudes and behaviours will determine our success or failure.

Do we want to continue this process of mind-control that has been, and still is, the root cause of our self-hatred and self-denial, with no way out? Or should we consciously retrain our minds to take responsibility for changing our attitudes and come together, using the veil of multi-culturalism to our advantage, and being determined to succeed at success?

The strategic plan of Willie Lynch has destroyed our lives, and the lives of our families, and will continue to affect us with each succeeding generation and government, in Canada, the USA, and all other countries around the world, and will continue, *if we do not take and make a conscious effort to change our thinking process.* **Attitude is what we think.**

Behavior is what we do.

Habits are what we do with what we think.

Only you can change your thinking. Your behaviours will manifest the changes you have made, and they will be continuous themes in your actions. Why not make sacrifices today, in order to overcome the negative conditioning we received from birth and carried with us in to the present?

This conditioning has caused us to develop habits of insecurity, inferiority complexes, poor judgment, and low self-esteem. By removing negative conditioning, and putting positive thinking habits in its place, we will be rewarded by seeing those you love (children and grandchildren) grow and change, as they respond to your positive changes, and you will grow, because they have changed and developed. This is the paradox of life. By consciously making these changes and committing them to permanency, you will experience all six of Abraham Maslow's "Hierarchy of Human Needs".

These needs begin with basic physiological things, like hunger, thirst, and so forth, followed by need for safety (to feel secure and safe from danger). Then you will feel a sense of belonging and being loved. Your need for esteem will be achieved as you affiliate with others, being competent and gaining approval and recognition in your society. As you work through and satisfy the above needs, you will develop potentialities to their fullest, as the self-actualizing process of developed living will begin. You will discover new freedoms and work hard at whatever you do. You will assume responsibility. You will be honest (avoiding pretenses or game playing). You will listen to your own feelings in evaluating experiences, rather than the voice of tradition.

Be prepared to make unpopular decisions, if your views don't coincide with those of most people.

Ultimately, you will be responsible for your life and actions, others around you, and the world's citizens.

Cited Work

Edelman, Peter, "Where Race Meets Class: The 21st. Century Civil Rights Agenda". Georgetown Journal on Poverty Law and Policy 12:1 (2005)

Gundersen, Craig and James P. Ziliak, "Poverty and Macroeconomic Performance across Space, Race and Family Structure." Demography (2004)

Fraser, George C., "Success Runs in Our Race", Publishers, William Morrow & Co., New York, N.Y (1994).

Krool, Andy. "What WE Don't Talk about When We talk about Jobs: The Continuing Scandal of African American Joblessness". New Labour Forum (Murphy Institute) (2012)

Hunt, Mathew, O. "Race/ Ethnicity and Beliefs about Wealth and Poverty". Social Science Quarterly (2004)

Chapter 9
Change and your Self-Image

People change for a number of reasons, but it is always through stimuli. Helen Perlman, who conducted research on change, found that in order for one to change, you need a balance between *discomfort and hope*. If you are unhappy or uncomfortable with your life and have no hope, you will not be motivated to change. However, if there is no discomfort in your life, and everything is fine, there is no motivation for change there either. Remember the principle of change. If you cannot identify the benefit, then there is no focus either.

By looking for the benefits in the changes you want to make, there are three types of change that affect us:

1. Neutral Stimuli

2. Positive Stimuli

3. Negative Stimuli

Neutral Stimuli

Neutral Stimuli are mild motivators. As an example: Life no longer appears to hold any challenges. So, you decide to make changes in your life, simply because you are bored.

Positive Stimuli

Positive stimuli are close cousins to neutral stimuli. Normally, when you are exposed or open to new experiences that excite and enthrall you, you may be enticed to change. For example: You learn to ski and find it so enjoyable that you decide to move to British Columbia, or you fall in love with someone who lives overseas and you decide to immigrate so the two of you can be together. You are enticed into changing through a positive influence.

Negative StimuliIn most cases, negative stimuli are prime motivators for wanting to change. Due to their emotional content, they are normally more readily acceptable and have more impact than the other two stimuli.

The reason for this acceptability can be found in one's upbringing and background. What we believe we can and cannot do is ingrained from a very early age. Parents are never taught how to be "parents". As a result, they do the best they can. Often, the end result is a lack of effective communication, and a tendency to communicate on an emotional level, rather than in a balanced way. With this balance missing, there is a risk that communication is incomplete, and there is a reliance on negativity.Example:

Parent: It's time to bathe.

Child: I just want to finish watching this TV program.

Parent: I said have your bath now!

Child: But why can't I___?

The child is normally faced with a response that is intolerant, impatient, and sometimes even threatening.

Rarely does a parent follow up with an alternative or intelligent reason for their request. It has been said many times that a child cannot be reasoned with. Following that advice will certainly establish a negative trend. This type of behaviour is carried forward into adult life, and adopted by many who play an influential or authoritarian role in our lives. It is not the intention to lay blame for all of our woes on our upbringing, but it would be remiss of us not to recognize the coalition between the influence of our childhood and our self-perception.

When your self-image is not intact, your ability to decipher fact from fiction is severely hampered. In these instances, fear, confusion, and a range of emotions normally initiate an under or overreaction. "Facts" are created, along with self-imposed limitations. This type of behaviour is carried forward and manifests itself in many diverse situations.

Example:

A young mother who "knows" she cannot have a career:

To justify this belief she cites:

- Lack of experience
- Lack of knowledge
- Numerous fears, i.e., fear of rejection, failure, etc.
- The old-fashioned idea that it's a "man's world"
- Lack of management skills
- Cannot leave her young children

All attempts to contradict these beliefs will be overridden by her self- perception.

It is incredible how expert we become at "knowing" what we can and cannot do.

It is a great pity that it will take either a negative or neutral stimuli to motivate this young woman into making changes and accepting responsibility. For example, if she divorces her husband or he passes away suddenly.

A television program interviewed half a dozen executives of large national and multi-national companies. They were all women. Two were in traditionally male-dominated industries. Each one had an amazing story to tell. One had been deserted by her husband and left alone to raise three children, with no money and no experience. Another was left in debt, and without a clue of what to do, when her husband suddenly passed away and left her with a failing company. These women, without any previous experience, both went on to become highly successful, developing their companies into large profit-making organizations despite the obstacles.

It took a huge negative upheaval to force change. Yet had the negative stimuli been removed, their ability to change their lives and develop their full potential would probably have gone unnoticed and unexplored.

Most people see a negative stimulus as the factor or cause of their disenchantment. Clearly, the above example indicates that the influence in itself is a catalyst. However, some sort of formula (either consciously or subconsciously) was used that allowed these women to achieve a position whereby they could act in their own best interest, within a Position of Autonomy.

Another example:

You hear through the grapevine that the company you work for must lay off a number of people. You fear that you will lose your job. Once again, we have an emotional situation, based on your perceptions, which will create excessive reactions, which (if not dealt with correctly) can lead to mistakes being made and successful resolutions jeopardized.

Some people might deal with the problem by quitting their job, simply because they are afraid of losing it. There are several alternatives to this emotional measure. Quitting is the least favourable.

When you receive negative stimuli, there is a tendency to allow your emotions to override your logical process.

BALANCING EMOTIONS AND LOGIC

Imagine you are on the ledge of a very steep cliff. To get to safety, you must climb off the ledge, but you cannot. You are afraid to move forward for fear of falling off, and afraid to climb back from where you came from. You know you have to do something about your present situation, but you become paralyzed with fear and indecision.

The result? You block *both* possibilities. You *accept* the circumstance as being beyond your control. Frustration builds and a pot -luck or random decision is made. Sometimes you attempt to do nothing. *Perhaps the problem will take care of itself.* Once you do this, there is clearly more trouble on the way, leaving you without any control!

TUNNEL VISION

You may feel that circumstances entrap you, and that fears dominate your decision-making process. Therefore, you feel that you cannot take responsibility for the situation or yourself.

Too often there is a tendency to consider negativism-criticism in an unfavourable light. These stimuli will initiate the idea that action must be taken, and the process of change has begun.

Nobody likes criticism; it is a negative stimulus. However, it is essential that you understand that, no matter what the motivator is, it is how you use the **information** and the end result that counts. You want a sense of control within these situations. We often forfeit this control, however, as we react to (rather than deal with) the circumstances. There is no substitute for taking responsibility. With this understanding, positive solutions and benefits can be found.

SENSITIVITIES

Often, when you get negative feedback, and you do not have the ability to listen, research, consider your own opinions, and weigh the pros and cons, you tend to look for ways to diminish the impact. You find excuses for it, or push the negativism away. You may even superficially agree, with words like "you have a point" but you block the change. You close your mind and remain exactly as you are. Most of us think and act as we do purely as a result of past experiences and influences in our lives. When you do this, you are not accepting responsibility, and therefore, take no action.

The process does not differ with positive stimuli. Positive reinforcement can be tremendous for your self-image! However, if you are functioning in the negative, you tend to be suspicious of feedback. When this happens, you begin to appreciate how much more complicated life becomes. Positive feedback, on the other hand, can boost your self-confidence. It can make you feel worthwhile, *if* you accept it. This brings us to an interesting question:

Should you allow others to influence you?

The simple answer is that you cannot help but be influenced by others. This information is not always favourable. At times, the influence is given erroneously. If you accept the responsibility to take control and create balance in your life, it is essential that you move to a *position of autonomy.*

What is the position of autonomy?

The position of autonomy is used to describe a process and a state. It is a unique method-attitude-technique, which will allow you to filter the stimuli and control your perceptions, without the risk of accepting only the facts you *consider appropriate or correct.* It is a feeling (a position) in which you feel responsible and comfortable with your decisions. It is a process that encourages you to interpret, rather than blindly accept or reject, stimuli, and it will encourage you to *take responsibility.*

The manner in which you act, and the decisions you make, will be consciously chosen by you.

However, if this is done *without* including the STOP CONCEPT, which is an emotional-management control trigger, you will have the following negative or ineffective results, caused by your emotional brain:

- **Step 1 - (Stop)** - You don't. You have your own opinion, so you do not recognize any need to stop.

- **Step 2 - (Listen)** - You are already listening to your own opinion, so you believe you are listening, and therefore, don't need to listen any more than you already are.

- **Step 3 - (Research)** - Why bother? You know the facts. You consider your own opinion as a credible substitute for actual input, so you don't feel the need to research anything.

- **Step 4 - (Update your opinion)** - Why? Your own opinion is already centre-stage, always reinforcing itself.

- **Step 5 - (Weigh the pros and cons)** - There is nothing to consider. You have already reached your conclusion.

- **Step 6 - (Define your objective)** - Your objectives have already been reached, based on your untested opinion.

- **Step 7 - (Go)** - You act, based solely on your emotional-brain reaction, without having included any logical input.

THE STOP CONCEPT AND MOVING TO YOUR POSITION OF AUTONOMY.

By visualizing a stop sign, you are able to use this method as a trigger device, forcing you to pause and consider the stimuli around you, allowing a physical process to condition you. By developing and using your **STOP CONCEPT**, you will be able to pause long enough to move to your Position of Autonomy (P.A.). This then gives you an opportunity to consider the alternatives, as opposed to blindly reacting to the stimuli around you. Your stop concept is used purely as a memo, interrupting the input and giving you more control over your emotions.

Through your Position of Autonomy, you pause and consider alternatives. Therefore, you use your Stop Concept to activate your P.A.

In the beginning, it is useful to shout the word STOP in your mind. It will activate a discipline, which will assist you in stopping. Remember, you are responsible for your own actions. We tend to allow our thoughts and emotions to dominate, and forget the fact that we can actually control our thinking and responses.

NOTE: Stopping is used as a discipline or memo device only. It then allows you to move to a P.A.

It is not the same as stopping and counting to ten, to keep from saying the wrong thing in the heat of the moment. This action only serves to stifle your emotions and reactions. The only reason you want to stop is so that you may move to a Position of Autonomy, which allows you to filter the stimuli and gain control. **POSITION OF AUTONOMY (P.A.)**

There are seven key areas that make up the structure of the P.A. They are as follows:

- The need to STOP
- The need to listen with a balanced view
- The need to do research and investigate
- The need to consider your own opinions
- The need to weigh the pros and cons and come up with your own conclusions
- The need to define your objective
- The need to take the requisite action

The Position of Autonomy is a filtration process. You want to balance your emotions with a correct mix of logical thought. You must accept that you want to become independent of extreme emotions within you, and the reactions which occur. These emotions are often triggered by what others *do or say.*

As an example: Jean is a very kind and generous person, who never says no to anyone who asks a favour of her. One morning, Jean was in the store, running an errand for her friend Joe, and was running late. She started getting very angry with Joe, for taking advantage of her good nature. *Why does he always do this to me?* she thought. *He's just using me. He never does anything for himself. He always gets other people to do things for him. He is selfish, and I am a fool for letting him ruin my day.*

Jean's anger was building and building. By the time she returned from the store, she was in a rage. Later, she told some friends that she was ready to storm over to Joe's office and berate him for always forcing her to disrupt her schedule to run his errands.

It was at this point that Jean, who (three-weeks earlier) had learned about the Position of Autonomy and the STOP CONCEPT, remembered to STOP. She told her friends what a revelation it was. Once she STOPPED, she was able to apply her emotional-management trigger. Without it, she was listening to her own opinion, governed by her emotional brain. She remembered that unchecked the emotional-brain's voice can be a damaging force, as it is saturated with opinion and emotions and contains very little logic.

Jean was able to conclude that Joe was not at fault. After all, she was the one who had offered to help in the first place. In future, she would not jump so quickly to do his errands, or if asked to do something that was not convenient, she would say no.

POSITIVE THINKING AND YOUR POSITION OF AUTONOMY

We have all heard of positive thinking and negative programming, but what does it mean? How is it used? Most explanations seem to describe a use or intent. A lot has been said about the **Power of the mind.** It is suggested that you merely "think positively," and then "*voila*"... all is supposedly well. The opposite to this, negative thinking, results in failure.

So, what is it that allows some of us to succeed where others fail? Why is it that one person can persevere through extreme difficulties and find solutions? What are they doing? What is the method or process they are using?

Within each of us is a power. It either reflects or absorbs energy. Consider for a moment how powerfully you restrain yourself from pursuing a goal or task, the inflexible strength you exert when you decide that you cannot do something! In reality, you are exerting an energy force or power. It certainly is not measurable; you can't see it or feel it. This power, however, in this instance, only serves to absorb your energy. It prevents you from achieving your desired goal. This becomes the opposite of your Position of Autonomy. With every negating phrase ("I can't) that you repeat to yourself, this force comes into play and your energies are absorbed.

To illustrate the point further, it is not common knowledge that elephants are relatively quick animals for their size. They can run approximately fifteen miles an hour. An elephant can also tear a huge tree, measuring almost a meter in circumference, out of the ground easily. So, how does one explain the fact that circus elephants are kept at bay by a very small peg placed in the ground?

The answer lies in the unquestioned perception the elephant holds. As a very young elephant, a comparatively huge peg and thick chain keep the animal in one place. Try as it might, the little elephant cannot succeed in pulling itself free. It accepts that it cannot do so. As the animal gets bigger, the size of the chain is enlarged to accommodate the elephant's leg, *but the peg remains the same size.*

The elephant never tests this limitation, because in it's mind it "*knows*" that it cannot pull out the peg.

Like the elephant, how often do you choose not to test or question your self-imposed limitations? With that choice, you do not allow all the facts to emerge. This is a one-sided approach with powerful restrictions imposed.

Only by moving to your Position of Autonomy, after stopping the myriad of stimuli, can you logically and neutrally attack the problem. Most "problems" are too emotionally charged. By using your P.A., you are able to consciously balance your emotions with logic.

You are not always aware of the detrimental effect your self-imposed limitations have on you, or the extent of the power you possess through your own fears. The problem lies in how easily you accept the status quo. The immense strength and power you exert over yourself goes unchallenged. With these factors in force, you are not attempting to reach your Position of Autonomy. You forfeit control, because you are not aware that you are using this power negatively.

Once you realize this power and its existence, you can use this energy, neutralize the negative effects, and consider your real options. Once you recognize that your passive resistance is in fact a powerful inhibitor, you can use your P.A. to challenge your perceptions, norms, and restrictions, and project your energies in a constructive manner.

Take the example of a Russian weightlifter who "knew" that he could not lift more than three-hundred kilograms. Many attempts were made—none successful. At the Olympic games, his trainers placed an extra three kilograms on his bar without his knowledge.

He knew he could lift three-hundred kilograms, so he did ... only to discover afterwards that he had broken a new world record by lifting three-hundred-and-three kilograms.

Had they told him of their intentions, the power that prevented him from lifting those three extra kilograms would only have increased, with his perception that he *could not do it*. You have to understand your situation. Your P.A. allows you to identify and focus on your objective in a balanced ethical manner, and to ***not focus on the obstacle***. Consider for a moment how easily you ***do not*** question your perceptions.

By moving to your Position of Autonomy, you will be acting in your best interests. Your initial reaction might be to say, "*But how do I do this?*" If this is your reaction, you are going wrong already by not accepting your own responsibility, in that you must be dependent mainly on yourself, thereby actively and consciously taking responsibility for your actions, which is a vital component. The alternative is to passively allow your actions (or non-action) to be determined by your emotions.

SELF IMAGE AND YOUR P.A.

Your self-image is like a road. This metaphorical road will take you through mountainous paths with dangerous declines, treacherous curves, and wide-open spaces to get lost in. Sometimes, the journey is mundane, sometimes it's exciting, and sometimes it's rough.

Think for a moment about what you need to assist you in finding your way: maps and road signs. Maps show you the direction to take after you decide where you want to go. Road signs tell you how fast to go, what town you are in, how to get there safely, how much farther you have to travel, etc. What do you consider to be the most important road sign? It is the stop sign. Without it, confusion and chaos would occur, and we would have no control.

In terms of your self-image and P.A., you need a discipline to enable you to balance and control the most influential factor in your life: perception. Through your ability to perceive, you fit the facts together and react accordingly. In other words:

PERCEPTION = FACT

These "facts" remain intact until your perception changes. What you need to assist you in controlling your perception is your P.A. What you need to move to the P.A. is a memo or control device—a trigger.

If you are driving along a long road in the middle of the Sahara Desert, and you come across a **STOP SIGN,** what would you do?

You would automatically do what you are conditioned to do: **STOP.**

When you come to a stop sign at an intersection, there is a controlled environment.

- **Consider your own opinions**
- **Weigh up all the pros and cons**

You are then filtering and interpreting. You are taking control and are responsible for your actions, which can now be planned and disciplined rather than reactionary and emotional. Balance your emotions with logic.

Chapter 9

USING YOUR P.A.

WHEN DO YOU USE YOUR P.A.?

Whenever your feelings (angry, despondent, tired, elated...) distort your understanding of a situation, and make you lose sight of your objective, this is the time to use your P.A. This often happens when you have a presumed knowledge or bias. Once these prejudices are in place, the whole concept of moving to your P.A. is lost. Once these perceptions are in place, you risk behaving in a spontaneous or instinctive manner that may not ultimately be in your best interests. Hence, it is important that you stop (STOP CONCEPT) the negative stimuli before you proceed.

To use the metaphor, imagine that your objective is a port or beacon towards which you are sailing. When your feelings cause heavy weather and fog, and turbulence threatens to throw you off course,

your P.A. will serve as both your compass and your sail.

Besides physical force, which is seldom used in a usual communication scenario, the only way another person can actually "force" you to do something is by playing on your emotions. This arsenal normally comprises of guilt, uncertainty, and confusion.

Even when someone else arouses your fears or desires, it is you who experiences them and determines to what extent you will let these factors influence you. Erratic decision-making, based on your emotions alone, creates an unfortunate circumstance in which you become your own worst enemy.

How can going to the P.A. benefit you?

Going to your P.A. has a number of benefits:

1. It puts you in control; you are taking responsibility.

2. It helps you prioritize your feelings, and therefore you are better able to cope with your emotions (balance).

3. It allows you to seek more than one solution/

4. It creates a forum for rational, logical, independent, and disciplined thinking.

By making yourself independent from your emotions, which are either aroused by others or by your own assumptions and perceptions, you can consciously take responsibility for your choices.

Your P.A. helps you prioritize your feelings.

The feelings you have in any given situation needn't be extreme in order to influence your behaviour.

For example: When you are asked whether you would like coffee or tea, you will express your preference for one or the other. In making that decision, you are examining how you feel about the two options.

A preference is an emotional evaluation on the like/dislike scale. Consequently, in making a decision between two options, you must be aware of your preferences and your perceptions. The coffee or tea example lacks emotion, and thus decision is easier to make. The more emotive the scenario, the more control is needed, but in principle, the rules remain unchanged.

You have the right to experience and express your feelings. When functioning from within your P.A., you do not want to suppress your emotions, nor do you want to let them take over. Through listening and researching, you become aware of your feelings and their influence on your thinking.

Your P.A. allows you to seek more than one solution.

One tends to react similarly to similar situations. You develop patterns of behaviour. Your P.A. allows you to consider alternative approaches.

As you understand your feelings and reactions in any given situation, you are better able to correctly focus and move towards your objective, directing your energies accordingly.

Your P.A. creates space for rational and disciplined thinking.

A main element is focus. The more emotional the situation is, the more you require rational input. A balance must be found between emotions and logic. Rationally examine the elements that determine your situation (such as your goal, the message, objective, limits, and the possible options of responses).

REFLECTION

(1) THE STOP CONCEPT AND MOVING TO YOUR P.A.

By visualizing a stop sign, you are able to use this method as a trigger device, forcing you to pause and consider the stimuli around you. You are, therefore, allowing a physical process to condition you. By developing and using your **STOP CONCEPT**, you will be able to pause long enough to move to your P.A. This then gives you an opportunity to consider the alternatives, as opposed to blindly reacting to the stimuli around you. Your STOP CONCEPT is used purely as a memo, interrupting the input and giving you more control over your emotions.

Through your Position of Autonomy, you pause and consider alternatives. Therefore, you only use your STOP CONCEPT to activate your P.A.

- The need to STOP

- The need to listen with a balanced view

- The need to do research and investigate

- The need to consider your own opinions

- The need to weigh the pros and cons and come up with your own conclusions.

- The need to define your objective

- The need to take the requisite action.

(2) WHEN DO YOU USE YOUR P.A.

Whenever your feelings distort your understanding of a situation and make you lose sight of your objective, this is the time to use your P.A. This often happens when you have a presumed knowledge or bias. Once these prejudices are in place, the whole concept of moving to your P.A. is lost. Once these perceptions are in place, you risk behaving in a spontaneous or instinctive manner that may not ultimately be in your best interests. Hence, it is important that you stop (STOP CONCEPT) the negative stimuli before you proceed.

Chapter 10
Revealing the New You

I'm sure you've discovered by now that changing your life isn't necessarily a complicated or difficult process, but it is one that requires vigilance and dedication. Your success in transforming your life will be directly proportional to how much you want to change. If you are serious about your work, and apply yourself, there is no possible way you'll come up short. Like anything else in life, adopting your new self-image doesn't come without paying a price, and the price is simply the time and effort you expend in taking control and causing the changes you desire. Let me talk about the process of change, what you are likely to experience as you continue down the path, and what you can realistically expect as far as the amount of time necessary to create the changes you desire.

I'm also going to share some new information concerning additional measures that may be very helpful in speeding up the process. Personal transformation is an ongoing process. It isn't done overnight. However, progress can be made overnight. You will reach your final target that quickly. Unfortunately, because many people tend to be impatient, this becomes a stumbling block. They unrealistically demand that they have what they want immediately or not at all. Such an attitude usually confirms the latter. They will not reach their goals. All this is especially true if someone desires sweeping, fundamental changes in his or her self-image.

Major changes by their very nature take some time to accomplish. Time is needed, first of all, to get started—to gather your energy and focus on what you want. Time is also required to break old habits and establish new ones. The principles covered here will hasten the process, but they are not going to magically transform your life, as though someone waved a magic wand over you. These are just simply tools, resources, and strategies, and as such, must be applied and work on. Experience and persistence are needed on your part in order for them to be most effective.

From the very outset, you would do well to accept the fact that some time and effort will be required for you to reach your ideal goal. For example: Many years ago, a source of discouragement that is occasionally faced by people starting down the path of personal transformation was voiced to me by a man I knew, named David.

"I just don't seem to be getting anywhere at all," he said. "I tried the things you've suggested, and I just don't seem to be progressing. Maybe I'm different from others, and I just can't get it." He was very discouraged and on the verge of giving up. He just wasn't progressing the way he thought he should.

This attitude poses some very serious questions, and addresses two important issues. What should you really expect, and how much time is required.? What you really expect, and how important it is, will determine your success. You should expect to be completely successful in changing any part of the life you desire. What you expect is exactly what you'll get. In an earlier chapter this was dealt with significantly.

What I want to mention here is that, although you should expect and desire your deepest and biggest dream, those expectancies should be tempered with the realization that you're going to have to work toward them. Some time is required to accomplish them. Does this mean that you won't reach them? Absolutely not. It only means that you're going to have to be patient. We start off in life crawling on all fours, and we wobble and fall many times in learning to walk, but eventually, we learn not only to walk but to run, roller skate, and dance.

What happens is that people often over generalize and misinterpret their efforts. They take setbacks or slow progress as indicators that they can't change or that they won't reach their goals. They stumble through faulty exercises in logic. Consider the following example: Someone is attempting to become more assertive, so he or she goes through mental-clearing sessions for positive beliefs. That person decided on some behavioural visualizations exercises, and then tries to carry through with them. But each attempt seems equally difficult. When the person tries to act assertively, he or she feels self-conscious and awkward with every attempt. After many attempts, with little apparent change, the person concludes, "This is impossible. I can't do it."

Now, such reasoning may seem logical at first. But it isn't ... and here's why it isn't, and how you can easily escape this very dangerous attitude: First of all, don't look upon your success based on whether or not you've achieved your ultimate goal. What might be your initial reaction to a statement like that? "That sounds crazy."

It isn't though. In fact, it's about the only way you won't get discouraged. Let me state this again: Don't base your success on whether or not you've achieved your ultimate goal. Look upon each attempt as a step *toward* reaching your goal, and as such, you will not be all that concerned with how successfully you perform, or how comfortable you felt. Rather, you will be focusing on the fact that you're *practising*. In fact, that you've taken one more step in the direction you want to go!

Your criteria for evaluation should be this: Did I try it? Did I force myself to act? Did I do it? If you answer affirmatively, then you succeeded. Period. Keep in the back of your mind the belief and conviction that, as you continue, you will reach your goal, regardless of what it is.

Secondly, realize that change normally follows a series of peaks and valleys. You might experience a sudden burst of success, followed by a period of slow progress. You might even possibly slide back downhill a little bit. But as you keep applying yourself, you will break free again and zoom further upward, or once again momentarily plateau. With this in mind, you really shouldn't be too surprised when you find yourself experiencing this rhythmical progression. If you think you've stagnated, trust that you have not. You have only temporarily levelled out. Don't misinterpret any experiences as proof that you can't continue. Changing in pace or levels are a natural part of the progression, inherent to almost any kind of change, be it self-transformation or something else. In response to people thinking they're not changing, I often tell them to consider deciduous trees. Through the winter, they drop their leaves, and they look like they're dead. They look like nothing is going on. Springtime comes around, and they still look like they're dead. Nothing is happening, but inside there *are* changes going on. If you were able to look inside of that tree, you would see the sap flowing up the trunk, and all of the other processes getting ready for the buds to burst forth, in just a very short while. So, though externally it looks like the tree is at a plateau, in actual fact, there are changes taking place within.

It the same with us. We move along for a while, making progress, and then it looks like were plateauing. It seems like we're not making progress, but there are things going on inside. Your subconscious mind is digesting and processing all of the things that have been going on. You're getting ready for your next growth spurt. Don't evaluate yourself on a daily or even a weekly basis. If you want to look at your progress, do it quarterly, in ninety-day intervals.

To make it a little more clear, consider the following example: When someone first learns to play a musical instrument, say guitar or piano, the student generally learns a great deal very rapidly after just one or two lessons. He or she learns some of the basic fundamentals, such as the names of the notes, time signatures, different rhythms counts, and beats per note. So, with this information, the student is able to play some very simple melodies fairly easily. But, as he or she progresses to more advanced material, the person usually experiences a period of slow improvement. The new material is more demanding, and requires a certain basic expertise, which the student is still learning. But with practice and more practice, the person makes a breakthrough and may quite suddenly discover that he or she is once again rapidly progressing. After a while, the student levels off again and progress slows. This process continues like this constantly. The same is true of internalizing your self-image. Progress will be incremental, and follow a pattern of sudden rises, followed by a gradual cooling off period to recognize the nature of change.

Thirdly, don't generalize, telling yourself that no matter how hard you are trying, you aren't making *any* progress. I assure you that you will always be making *some* improvements, even though, at times, the improvements may seem to be small or gradual.

There was a friend of mine who experienced a broken romance. He confided in me that, no matter how hard he tried, he just couldn't shake his attachment to his girlfriend. He described himself as feeling depressed and miserable a lot of the time. When I pressed him about it, he quickly realized that this wasn't really altogether true. I asked him, "Do you think that you can feel good about yourself for half an hour each day?" "Of course," he said. "After all, half an hour's not long."

"Well, why don't you concentrate on feeling good for an additional five minutes every day," I suggested. "If you can progress five minutes per day, or longer, you'll feel better about yourself more often than you feel miserable."

You see what I'm getting at. If you just think that you aren't advancing, take a moment to really evaluate your situation. Look for the very smallest moment of successes if you have to, but find it. It will be there. If you're accomplishing your objective for just one minute a day, that's progress. Each day, add more time. Tell yourself, "Today I'll be filled with strong positive self-esteem for five whole minutes." And then add more time the next day, and so on. Small increments build up a lot faster than you might think. It is by doing this that you get your mind off failure and on to success. It causes you to concentrate on your objective, and helps you develop confidence. You're progressing forward as you gain confidence. Your growth will then greatly accelerate.

The second question everyone wants answered is this: How much time will it take for me to accomplish my goal? Now the answer I am going to give you may sound like a cop-out, but it takes as much time as it will take. Now, I know that's not really what you wanted to hear, but it's really the only accurate answer I can give. Each person is different. Each individual is unique. Some people take readily to change and advance toward their goals quite rapidly, but for others, any kind of change is difficult and requires more time and work. Because of this unavoidable reality, there simply isn't any formula that you can use that will tell you exactly how long you're going to have to wait. or exactly how much effort you're going to have to expend. Those things are determined by each individual situation. There are, however, some very basic factors that can be indicative.

First of all, transformation of character traits tends to take the most amount of time and energy. For instance, if you're developing patience, but you've been inpatient all your life, you will be making a change to your basic nature, and this require a little bit more time. You have to break the old habit, and then learn a new one. If the old habit is one that you've had for years, then both time and effort will be required to replace it with a more desirable one.

Secondly, determination and persistence make an immense difference. If you're zealous and energetic about your goal, you are going to reach it a lot quicker. On the other hand, if you really aren't all that committed to it or determined, then you should expect a longer haul. Finally, your willingness to accept and try new ideas might be a big factor. By this, I mean that if you have been open-minded toward suggestions and techniques, and you're really willing to give them an honest effort, you're going to change a lot more rapidly than someone who allows doubt and skepticism to sabotage his or her efforts.

To establish a frontal assault on building a positive self-image, utilize all your tools daily, month after month, and soon you will be amazed at the new you. Actually, if you're overly concerned with how much time changing your self-image will take, you are focusing your energy in the wrong place. The only thing that should matter, and the only thing you really should be concentrating on, is the fact that you can, are, and will continue to advance toward your goal. As you commit yourself to transforming your life, there are additional easy measures you can take that will help you greatly reinforce all the exercises I have covered with you.

I want to cover all these with you, and end with a final example, showing just how much someone can change, if that person is dedicated and serious. Almost all psychologists agree that some types of physical benefits are often helpful in inspiring people to break unwanted routines and change their behaviour. There are number of different things that fit this category. One that you might consider is fashion. There is a curious magic about clothing that can actually affect the way you feel about yourself. For instance, when facing a stressful situation, such as a job interview or an important meeting, clothing styles can actually help you feel more confident. Many behavioural therapists believe that clothing can be used to alter mood, and even recommended the purchase of new clothing to certain depressed clients. Naturally, there are no specific kinds of clothing that always produce a given result, because taste in clothing is highly personal. Styles that help one person to feel confident or loving or self-assured may have no effect (or the opposite effect) on the next person. You might also consider that others often form impressions of us based on our style of dress. We are expected to draw certain conclusions about a person's identity based on clothing. Unlike other personal possessions, such as a wallet or purse or home furnishings, clothes are highly visible, and alive with information about the wearer.

They contain a wealth of clues concerning who the person is or isn't, and who they want to be.

With all this in mind, take some time to evaluate whether or not your clothing style reinforces the self-image you're developing. If you're striving to become a self-confident businessperson, for example, make sure your dress conveys that image. So what you wear really can make a difference. It doesn't only make a difference in how others see you. It can make a big difference in how you feel about yourself, which is even more important.

If you have to go out and buy some new clothes, you won't be disappointed. And along the same lines, changing hairstyle or sometimes even colour can also help. Focus on change. Altering the hairstyle or colour of itself doesn't really make you change, but it can become a catalyst to help you think and feel differently about yourself. The physical act of changing clothing fashion or hairstyles helps you concentrate on change. Your outward physical actions are reinforcing your inner-conviction. They help convince yourself that you're serious. You mean business. Breaking old habits and routines may also help. This will serve to shift your mind off any temporary problems or setbacks that you might be facing. Breaking routines will often give you new perspective, not only on any troublesome situation but on life in general.

There are many different ways to climb out of ruts and break routine. Try a new activity. Taking up a new hobby is an effective, rewarding, and fun way to do. Try to find some hobby or activity that reinforces the self-image you are developing. For instance, if you're working on leadership, why not join some civic organization or church organization where you can take advantage of any opportunities to help with things like various committees, where you can practice your leadership skills? If you're interested in becoming a successful and confident businessperson, you might want to join a professional organization, where you can associate with others who are successful and confident.

On the other hand, joining groups or clubs may not be your style. Perhaps you find it helpful to take up a sport or an outdoor activity, which that would be especially helpful if you're striving to become more athletic or physically fit. Being physically fit also influences how a person feels about him or herself. Breaking routines can also be as simple as going to a movie when you normally wouldn't, or going out for dinner at an odd time. Any change in pace is often very helpful in broadening your perspective, and giving you a fresh new look at life. The possibilities for different kinds of things you can do to break the constraints of routine are really limitless. Spend a few moments on introspection occasionally, to determine what would be best for you, and then (of course) do it.

Some people I've worked with over the years really don't have any conviction that it's possible to dramatically alter their lifestyle or basic character traits. They feel that all someone can hope for is to work with what he or she really has and try to make the best of it. If you are thinking that way ... don't. Such thinking is wrong. You have the power to completely transform your life any way you want to. You are only limited by your desire, persistence, and imagination. Whatever your dream and hope for can be yours, if you want it badly enough.

In conclusion, let me share an example of someone who did not allow negative thinking to interfere with his plans. Someone who saw possibilities rather than limitations. Someone who preferred action rather than inaction. This person is no different than anyone else. What he did you can do. Here's the story:

This man really wasn't very happy with his life, and he wanted to change it. He was tired of compromising his goals and his ideals. He wanted more from life, so he decided to take control and start changing things. He thoroughly analyzed his entire life, and chose the kind of person he wanted to be. Then got busy becoming that person. His zealousness and convictions spared him no rest. To begin, he spent a lot of time each and every day doing visualizations and positive affirmations concerning his ideal self-image. But he wasn't content to limit his efforts to strictly mental exercises. True to himself, he realized how important those things were, but he was so enthusiastic about changing that he sought other avenues that would help. He knew that, by implementing major physical changes, he would strongly reinforce the new beliefs and ideas he had internalized about himself.

So, he stepped boldly forward and altered his life on virtually every physical level he could think of. He changed his hairstyle, adopted a different style of clothing, moved half way across the city to an upscale neighbourhood, changed his job, and become a business consultant. He still wasn't satisfied.

He had one thing left to do, and he did it without blinking an eye. He attended university and obtained a Doctor of Philosophy degree, even more deeply and effectively breaking any remaining ties to his old identity, and further reinforcing the new image by adding "doctor" to his name. By making a total commitment, sparing no effort, this individual was successful in completely transforming himself into a loving, positive, confident, and very successful person. It is an incredible transformation to behold.

I've known this person now for all of my life, and I can tell you that the degree of change is phenomenal. It has been like knowing two different people. Well, I'm not suggesting that you necessarily follow this person's example to the letter. For most people, changing jobs, location etc. may not serve an important purpose. The intent of this example is to show you that there are no limits to the degree and amount that you can change. Set your own limits. You can make slight adjustments, or you can totally transform yourself into a truly 100 percent different person. It's up to you, and what you want to do. No one else can do it. Only you can. You can become anything you dream of becoming. You can exert complete control over your life. What a fantastic promise of freedom! The freedom to do, to be, and to become whatever your imagination directs you toward!

I wish you much success and happiness as you reach toward your desired new self-image.

REFLECTION

(1)   All major changes, by their very nature, take some time to accomplish. Time is needed first of all, to get started, to gather your energy and focus on what you want, and to break old habits and establish new ones.

(2)   Two important issues to be addressed are what you should really expect, and how much time is required. What you really expect is very important, because it will determine your success. You should expect to be completely successful in changing any part of the life you desire. What you expect is exactly what you'll get.

(3)   Please don't generalize - People often generalize and misinterpret their efforts. They take setbacks or slow progress as indicators that they can't change, and that they won't reach their goals. They stumble through faulty exercises in logic.

(4)   Don't base your success on whether or not you've achieved your ultimate goal. Look upon each attempt as a step toward reaching your goal, so that you will not be all that concerned with how successful you perform, or how comfortable you felt. Instead, you will be focusing on the fact that you're practising, and have taken one more step in the direction you want to go.

(5)   Realize that change normally follows in a series of peaks and valleys. You might experience a sudden burst of success followed by a period of slow progress.

(6)   Determination and persistence make an immense difference. If you're zealous and energetic about your goal, you are going to reach it a lot quicker.

(7)   At times, you will not feel up to the task, but there are many different ways to climb out of ruts and break routine. Try

new activities. Taking up a new hobby is an effective, reward-ing, and fun way to do this. Try to find some hobby or activity that reinforces the self-image you are developing.

Acknowledgements

This work would not have been done without the assistance and guidance of my family, many friends, and associates. A special thanks to my wife—who believed in me and encouraged me to get the book completed—for her patience during the long hours I spent writing.

Also, big thanks to Professor Donald (Don) Williams, who with his exchange of ideas and encouragement, was instrumental in me writing this book. My many students at Humber College, Business Communication Class, I owe you a great deal of gratitude for allowing me to share my thoughts and ideas about change, and how it affects your self-image in the communication process.

To my daughter, Vanessa Simpson, you have made me proud by going over chapters eight and nine, and sharing ideas on how to improve them. Michael Nawar and Brinsy Nickie, I thank you both for your contribution and feed-back on various chapters. In addition, my thanks and appreciation go to many colleagues who have entrusted me with their thoughts and opinions.

I have benefited immensely from the inspiration and sage advice of the editors and publishing specialists at FriesenPress. I Thank you.

And to Gloria Joyette, I owe a tremendous debt of gratitude for the faith you had in me and my ability to complete this project, and for your encouragement every step of the way. You read the entire manuscript, and shared thorough and meaningful dialogue, and insights on how to improve and better express my ideas. I thank you.

Finally, my thanks and appreciation to the entire Joyette family, for allowing me a front-row seat from which I had the opportunity to see, learn, and experience the inner-dynamics of their thoughts, behaviours, and actions.

Bibliography

Begley, Sharon, (2007) Train your Mind, Change your Brain, Ballantine Books. New York, N.Y.

Buechner, Frederick (1991) The Sacred Journey, HarperCollins Publishers, New York, N.Y

Brown, Les (1991) Take Time to Dream - Turn your dream into reality, ABS, Inc. USA

_____ Les (1991) Fear and Failure - Overcome Fear and Determine your Future, ABS, Inc. USA

_____Les, (1991) Your Greatest Investment - Long Term Dividend with Personal Success, ABS, Inc. USA

Cialdini, Robert. B (2007) Influence - The Psychology of Persuasion, HarperCollins Publishers, New York, N.Y.

Duhigg, Charles (2014) The Power of Habit, Anchor Canada Publishers, Canada

_____, Charles (2016) Smarter Faster Better, Doubleday Publishers, Canada

Fraser, George. C.(1994) Success Runs in Our Race, William Morrow & Co., New York, N.Y

Lorenz, Konrad (1965) Evolution and Modification of Behavior, University of Chicago Press, Chicago

Scott, Peck. M. (1978) The Road Less Travelled, Touchstone-Simon & Schuster Inc. New York, N.Y

_____ (1993) Further Along the Road Less Travelled, Touchstone, New York, N.Y. USA

_____ (1997), The Road Less Travelled and Beyond, Touchstone, New York, N.Y. USA

Printed in Canada